The Art of the Router

The *Art* of the Router

Award-Winning Designs

Patrick Spielman

Sterling Publishing Co., Inc. New York
A Sterling/Chapelle Book

Chapelle Ltd.

Owner: Jo Packham

Design/layout Editor: Leslie Ridenour

Staff: Marie Barber, Areta Bingham, Malissa Boatwright, Kass Burchett, Rebecca Christensen, Holly Fuller, Marilyn Goff, Shirley Heslop, Holly Hollingsworth, Susan Jorgensen, Leslie Liechty, Pauline Locke, Ginger Mikkelsen, Barbara Milburn, Linda Orton, Karmen Quinney, Rhonda Rainey, and Cindy Stoeckl

Technical drawings: Roxanne Lemoine and Lorna Johnson

On the Cover: Jeff Greenup's Library Step, Honduras mahogany with cocobolo accents, 56" H x 20" radius of step x 8", 16", and 24" tread heights

On page 2: Barry LaChance's All Buttoned Up or The Seeing Eye Table: dual pedestal table, American white oak with oak burl inlay

Note: Since photographing for this book, Jesada Tools changed the color of their line of router bits. The bits are no longer available in orange, but can now be found in white.

Library of Congress Cataloging-in-Publication Data

Spielman, Patrick E.
    The art of the router : award winning designs / Patrick Spielman.
       p. cm.
    Includes index.
    "A Sterling/Chapelle book."
    ISBN 0-8069-4285-1
    1. Routers. (Tools) 2. Woodwork. I. Title.
TT203.5.S623 1998
683'.083--dc21
                              97-44394
                                CIP

10 9 8 7 6 5 4 3 2 1

A Sterling/Chapelle Book

Published by Sterling Publishing Company, Inc.
387 Park Avenue South, New York, NY 10016
© 1998 by Chapelle Ltd.
Distributed in Canada by Sterling Publishing
% Canadian Manda Group, One Atlantic Avenue, Suite 105
Toronto, Ontario, Canada M6K 3E7
Distributed in Great Britain and Europe by Cassell PLC
Wellington House, 125 Strand, London WC2R 0BB, England
Distributed in Australia by Capricorn Link (Australia) Pty Ltd.
P.O. Box 6651, Baulkham Hills, Business Centre, NSW 2153, Australia
Printed in Hong Kong
All Rights Reserved

Sterling ISBN 0-8069-4285-1

Due to limited amount of space available, we must print our patterns at a reduced size in order to give our patrons the maximum number of projects possible in our publications. We believe the quality and quantity of our patterns will compensate for any inconvenience this may cause.

If you have any questions or comments or would like information about any specialty products featured in this book, please contact:

Chapelle Ltd., Inc.
P.O. Box 9252
Ogden, UT 84409

Phone: (801) 621-2777
FAX: (801) 621-2788

Patrick Spielman

Patrick Spielman lives surrounded by a national forest in the famous tourist area of Door County in northeast Wisconsin. A graduate of the University of Wisconsin-Stout, he taught high school and vocational woodworking in Wisconsin public schools for 27 years.

Patrick's love of wood and woodworking began between the ages of eight and 10, when he transformed fruit crates into toys. Encouragement from his parents, two older brothers, and a sister, who provided basic tools to keep the youngster occupied, enabled Patrick to become a very productive wood-worker at quite an early age.

Today, he and his wife, Patricia, own Spielman's Wood Works and Spielman's Kid Works. Both are gift galleries that offer high-quality hand- and machine-crafted wood products produced locally and from around the world.

Patrick left the school classroom more than 10 years ago, but he continues to teach and share ideas and designs through his published works. He enjoys consulting and lending his knowledge of woodworking to promote the talent and activities of other artisans. He has written more than 50 woodworking books with some translated into Dutch and German.

One of Patrick's proudest accomplishments is his book, *The Router Handbook*, which sold more than 1.5 million copies worldwide. His updated version, *The New Router Handbook*, was selected the best how-to book of 1994 by the National Association of Home and Workshop writers.

Patrick has made a number of appearances on public television and he continues to serve as a technical consultant and designer for a major tool manufacturer.

He and his family recently formed Spielman Publishing Co. for the purpose of publishing and distributing "Home Workshop News," a color bi-monthly newsletter dedicated to scrollsawing, small router projects, and general related woodworking activities.

A new title by Patrick, *Artistic Scroll Saw Projects*, has just been released and he is currently at work on two more new books of projects and patterns for scroll sawing.

Acknowledgements:

My sincerest appreciation and warmest thanks to each of the featured router artists who kindly provided projects, photographs, drawings, and descriptive copy of their works.

I also wish to extend my gratitude to other individuals who have helped in a variety of ways. First, and always, thank you to my wife, Patricia, for her support and continued tolerance of my work commitments.
The following people have generously provided information, illustrations, and assistance which has a very definitive impact on this book: Carlo and David Venditto and Cliff Paddock of Jesada Tools; Ken and Mathew Grisley of Leigh Industries Inc.; Jim Phillips of Trend Machinery and Cutting Tools, Ltd.; Tracy Anderson of Phantom Engineering Inc.; Chris Taylor of Taylor Designs; Greg Powell of Jacobs Chuck Mfg. Co.; and Carter Williams of DeWalt Industrial Tool Co.

Others who have also helped along the way include: Phil Adams, Hank Bardenhagen, Jim Box, Dick Jarmon, David Keller, Julie Kiehnau, Barbara and Harvey Malzahn, J. P. Poulan, Fred Salerno, Robert Spielman, Jim Vinella, Walt Vinoski, Dan Walter, Pat Warner, and Wally Wilson.

Introduction

This book is a visual display of creative expression in woodworking involving the use of the router. The high speed and cutting efficiency of the router leave it standing alone in its versatility and value to woodworking artists. Not only used for obvious decorative surface and edge work, the router also handles much of the utilitarian and functional aspects of the woodworker's art as well. Sometimes the router's contribution in an artistic piece is never seen, but remains hidden in various structural elements and supplemental joint work.

The uncomplicated exactitude of router cutting, however, has nourished the popularity of exposed decorative joinery. Throughout this book there are examples of mortises, finger joints, pin and cove, and some very ornate dovetails. Some may be more pretentious than artistic, but all are superbly executed.

Many prominent woodworking artists have fashioned stylish furniture and various household accessories and adornments with their mastery of the router. Several examples herein unite art and utility as plain wood is transformed into beautiful, original treasures. These one-of-a-kind creations will never grow old, will never become useless, nor turn the eye away unsatisfied.

Sometimes it may be that the artistry is not in the final piece but in the brilliance of jig or template design and the planning that enabled the artisan to dispatch the router to various desired tasks. However, the router is only the carrier of the bit—the tool that does the actual cutting. The router is nothing until it is loaded with the chosen bit and deftly applied to the workpiece. Each artisan has their own personal preference for routers and favorite bit configurations. The woodworker tutors himself as each new piece offers another experience and another challenge.

The various pieces designed and provided by the artisans for this book are meant to be studied and used for personal inspiration and enrichment. Splendid photographs clearly illustrate each artist's choices of structural elements and their favorite species and colors of woods. Pairing these visual images with individual biographical sketches affords the reader personal insight as to what stimulates or inspires each gifted woodworker. Think of this book as an opportunity to work under a panel of excellent router masters and, in turn, expand and enrich future personal experiences with the router.

Patrick Spielman, 1998

Contents

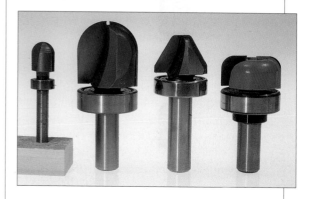

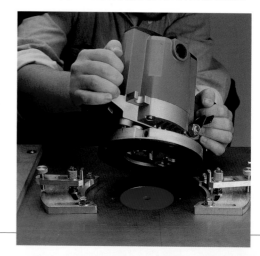

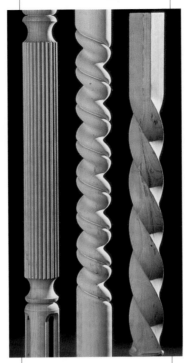

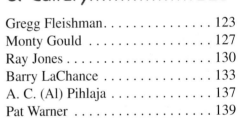
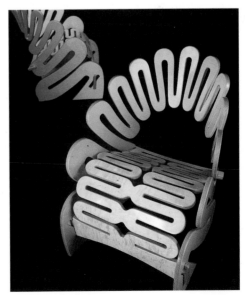

Early Routers

The electric hand router has been around for 95 years or more. As early as 1905 the first commercially produced router was marketed by the Kelly Machine Co. of Buffalo, New York. See **Photos No. 1-1 and 1-2**. Although the Kelly router was very crude and heavy, it instantly became the revolutionary development for the wood-working trades—especially the furniture and architectural millwork industries. The router eliminated tedious hand carving and made correct geometrical cuts. A testimonial letter in an early Kelly Catalog stated, ". . . for fluting columns and pilasters (Kelly's) machine cannot be beat." Kelly's advertising motto boldly read, "Clean finished cuts in straight or cross grain." Notice in the photos how the base housing and the rub collar above the bit are similar to present day designs.

Around 1914, Carter routers, manufactured in Phoenix, New York, appeared and quickly earned the designation of "Wonder Tool." They were considerably smaller than the Kelly routers, but their 1½ H.P. model still weighed 35 pounds. Carter routers featured a threaded motor housing depth adjustment system and many other features that are essentially still the same as found on some present day routers. Edge guides, base mounted template guides, D-handles, bits from ¹⁄₁₆" to 1" were likewise similar to those available today. Carter patented a dovetail template system in 1927, but records show an earlier patent was granted in Germany for a dovetail system in 1906.

Photo No. 1-1 and 1-2. One of the first electric routers. This three-phase Kelly router was manufactured in 1905. It weighed 60 pounds, was more than 12" in diameter and 16" high. *Photos courtesy: Walt Vinoski.*

1-1

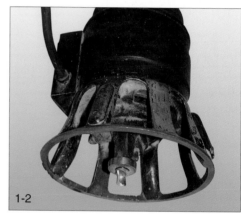

1-2

Photo No. 1-3. Forerunners of the Porter-Cable routers. Right is an earlier UNIQUIP Model C and on the left is one of the first Speedmatics®, circa mid-1940s. *Photo courtesy: Dick Jarmon.*

1-3

Stanley Electric Tools purchased the Carter line in 1929 and produced routers until the company was sold to the Bosch Tool Corp. in the early 1980s.

Forerunners of the popular Porter-Cable fixed-base routers, circa mid-1940s, are shown in **Photo No. 1-3**.

The plunge router didn't arrive on the scene until 1949 when developed by Elu in Germany. Elu routers became known throughout the world as the best and set a standard for all other plunge routers. Interest in plunge routers in the U.S., however, was fairly non-existent until the early 1980s. In recent years Elu was purchased by Black and Decker who also owns DeWalt Industrial Tool Co. Today, the DeWalt plunge routers are still made in Europe and are direct clones of the famous Elu plunge routers. Elu fixed base routers are made in the United States. Otherwise, distribution of Elu brand routers in the U.S. has been discontinued.

Routers Today

A recent count revealed nearly 100 different routers available today from 14 manufacturers. There are many very good routers available, far more than can be listed here. See **Photos No. 1-4 through 1-7**. For an in-depth discussion of router accessories and techniques, refer to the author's book, *The New Router Handbook*.

There are now more choices in plunge routers than the fixed base type in the U.S. and it appears that this trend will continue. The one aspect of the fixed base router that may be an important advantage is the fact that usually the motor can be removed from the base and used independently in other

Photo No. 1-4. Sears has three light duty ¼" routers priced under $100 and two industrial, ½" models.

Photo No. 1-5. The Bosch line offers a choice of 12 routers and six laminate trim routers. This popular variable speed model is available in 1 and 2 HP models with ¼" and ½" chucks respectively.

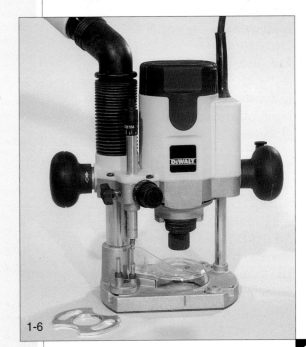

Photo No. 1-6. DeWalt industrial plunge routers are clones of the famous European Elu line. This 2 HP, ½" variable speed model, the newest of four available, features an innovative dust extraction through the larger plunge column.

fixturing or accessories as shown in **Photo No. 1-8**.

Desirable Router Features

In addition to fixed base verses plunge type routers, there is also a choice between ¼" and ½" maximum collet size capacities. See **Photo No. 1-9**. A broader selection of bits is available with ½" shanks rather than ¼". But for certain jobs light routers are preferred because of their light weight and ease of operation with one hand.

As a general rule, the deeper the inside opening or overall length of the collet the better. See **Photo No. 1-10**. Good collets also have more linear splits to grab the bit more uniformly around the shank. And, collets should be made of tempered, hardened steel. Test them with a file. If it makes a cut, the collet is not tempered, but soft which is not good. For general purpose work, ½" collet routers are recommended. Large routers up to 3½ H.P. are available for industrial/continuous use. Spindle locks and self releasing collets (pulls the bit out as the nut is loosened) are nice features, but not found on all routers.

The switch should operate easily and, preferably, from the handle or it should be located within reach without needing to remove the hand from the knob or handle.

The design of the base offers more design choices. Some are not completely round but have combined straight and circular edges as shown in **Photo No. 1-11**. This may allow for working closer to a vertical obstruction. It may also make following a straight edge easier. Meanwhile, larger round bases have more surface area supporting the router and can bridge larger openings.

Photo No. 1-7. The author's favorite style of fixed-base router is this D-handle type. Shown here is a 2½ HP ½" design by Porter-Cable who also offers eleven different routers including three plunge models and a variety of small trimmer units.

Photo No. 1-8. A fixed-base router offers the advantage of removing the motor unit from the base and using it for special shop made fixturing or accessory devices such as router carving machines and the like.

Photo No. 1-9. Bigger is better when it comes to collet sizes and the router's capability to carry bits with large shanks. Notice how much stronger and stiffer the ½" shank looks than the same cutter on the ¼" shank.

Photo No. 1-10. A good collet is one important measure of router quality; the longer the better and the more splits the better.

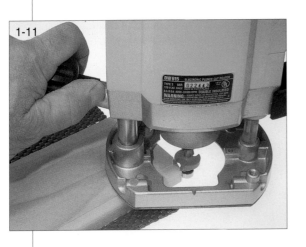

1-11

It is important to consider whether there is provision for interchanging various styles of sub-bases. See **Photos No. 1-12 through 1-15**. For general shop use, it is also important that the base have sufficiently threaded sockets that allow safely hanging the router inverted for table use. Refer to **Chapter 4: Router Saftey Precautions** on page 25.

The depth of cut adjustment and locking clamp should be quick and easy to operate with a fine adjustment provision. See **Photos No. 1-16 and 1-17**. A plunge router intended for use in a router table should be equipped with a depth control knob for easy adjustment or this accessory should be available. See **Photo No. 1-18**.

Other important features include overall quality construction, good bearings, durable brushes, and new electricals such as soft starts and the variable speed option. Also check the avail-ability and mounting convenience of template guides, edge guides and the adaptability of the router as a power source for other machinelike accessories such as router lathes, carving machines, or other special router driven joinery devices.

Photo No. 1-11. Some routers have small bases which tend to make them tippy. Notice the big central opening and how little of the base is actually supporting this router as the operator turns the corner during this frequently performed task of routing an edge.

Photo No. 1-12. Pat Warner manufactures this replacement base accessory which provides sufficient support for performing the same operation more safely and accurately.

1-12

Photo No. 1-13. The author's trim router fitted with a special base featuring a hole with almost zero clearance around the bit—essential for routing small parts.

1-13

Photo No. 1-14. Rounding over a small part on a non-slip router pad, work that could not be done otherwise, especially if using a larger router with a big bit opening like the one shown in Photo No. 1-11.

1-14

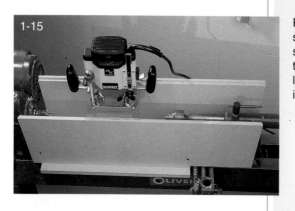

1-15

Photo No. 1-15. A square plastic base supports and guides the router on this lathe fixture for fluting straight turnings.

1-16

Photo No. 1-16. A spring loaded depth of cut lock/release lever on this Bosch router is one of the easiest to use. It automatically clamps upon release.

Photo No. 1-17. The plunge depth lock and release on the new 2 HP DeWalt router is accomplished by twisting the left knob.

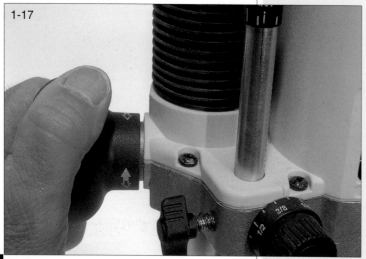

1-17

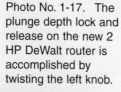

Photo No. 1-18. A depth of cut control knob is an excellent feature/accessory for inverted table routers.

1-18

Future Routers

According to leading experts, some very exciting innovations will appear before the next century. Look for quick change collets which will not require a spindle lock or wrenches. See **Photos No. 1-19 through 1-22**. This is a major breakthrough! It is from the Jacobs Chuck Mfg. Co., the 1990 inventors of the keyless drill chucks. This new device is called the "Hand-Tite® Routerchuck™ Collet System." The first products will be available on just ¼" collet capacity routers with ½" sizes expected to follow shortly. These new collets will "enable the user to install a bit in seconds by releasing the sleeve, replacing the bit and snapping the sleeve back into the locked position." The concept is somewhat similar to the device that grips the lead of a mechanical pencil. Models will also eventually be available as add-ons to

existing ½" collet routers. These will have a round shank that fits into an existing collet. See **Photo No. 1-22**. These add-ons may create some problems for depth adjustments with hand-held routers, but may also be an advantage for routers installed in tables by providing additional reach. According to the manufacturer, preliminary tests indicate that there will be no significant increase in run out or vibration.

Also coming are dust collection devices that do not require an external vac, but will be powered by the fan on the motor. Look for more comfortable ergonomic design for one-hand use on smaller routers. "The trend is toward total dust-free, hassle-free routing. The future promises a refinement of existing motor technology including better speed controls, soft starts, and brakes on all routers. Look for longer lasting brushes, double wound motors, heavy duty switches, metal housings where needed with stronger plastics (glass filled nylon), all intended to make

Photo No. 1-19. The revolutionary Hand-Tite® Router-Chuck™ quick change collets will not require wrenches or a spindle lock for bit installation. *Photo courtesy: Jacobs Chuck Mfg. Co.*

routers more durable as well as more comfortable. There will also be rubber grips, so sweaty hands won't slip, and handle designs that are comfortable at any work angle."

U.S. manufacturers will need to look to Europe for router forecasting.

Photo No. 1-20. A closer look at the new collet. *Photo courtesy: Jacobs Chuck Mfg. Co.*

Photo No. 1-21. Detail of the Router-Chuck gripping action. *Courtesy: Jacobs Chuck Mfg. Co.*

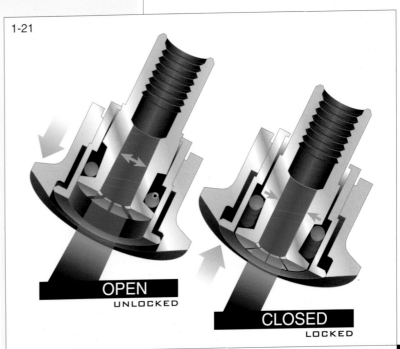

OPEN
UNLOCKED

CLOSED
LOCKED

Fixed base routers are essentially illegal in most countries in Europe. The plunge router offers a level of safety that fixed base routers cannot offer. The springs of the plunge router return a dangerously exposed bit into the relatively protected confines between the plunge rods. A plunge router can do almost everything a fixed base router can do, but still, a fixed base router can only be a fixed base router.

Europe is also ahead with regard to controlling dust. The largest producer of uncontrolled dust in the shop is the router. Europe is leading the charge for better dust control. Stricter dust control regulations are also being more aggressively enforced in the U.S. Production shops will soon be forced to do a better job of collecting dust at the point of cut—routers included.

Photo No. 1-22.   A Hand-Tite® chuck will be a welcomed convenience for router table users.

1-22

Chapter 2: Router Bits

In recent years manufacturers have made enormous strides in the technological improvement of router bits. Today router cutters are sharper, longer lasting, and safer in design. The choices of new cutting profiles continues to grow at huge numbers. In the midst of all these advances, however, there are still some poor quality and potentially dangerous bits being offered to the vulnerable buyer. See **Photo No. 2-1**.

This chapter will focus on important characteristics to look for in selecting quality router bits. It will also take a brief look at some samples of bits available. Books and manufacturer's catalogs often offer more choices in sizes and profile designs than perhaps one needs to see.

Photo No. 2-1   The peril of using a poor quality or dull bit. The bottom sample shows an inside corner burn that is almost impossible to correct without destroying the integrity of the shape and the labor involved would be excessive.

2-1

Anti-Kickback Design

One of the most notable and important advances of the 90s was the introduction of the European safety style bits to the U.S. See **Photo No. 2-2**. Carlo Venditto, President of Jesada Tools of Oldsmar, Florida was the first to introduce a full line of these bits in 1991. As other manufacturers have unloaded their inventories, many are changing over to produce the new safety style bits. These new cutters feature a larger and heavier body than the older style. The body, however, is slightly smaller than the overall cutting diameter which defines the anti-kickback feature. The body limits the "bite" of the cutter on each revolution so the chance of a kickback is minimal. Because of the greater mass, these bits dissipate heat away from the cutting edge better. And, because they are also heavier they minimize chatter and vibration. As with any bit, however, it must be sharp and balanced.

Checking Sharpness

Some brand new bits are not always sufficiently sharp. In fact, some are ground so poorly imperfections can be detected with the naked eye. See **Photo No. 2-3**. Use a magnifying glass when checking the smoothness of the grind. The surfaces should be smooth and polished. The end of a fingernail is sensitive enough to help detect coarse grinds not visible with the naked eye. Simply slide the end of the nail down the face or along the back bevel of the edge as shown in the **Photo No. 2-4**. A sharp edge will also shave the surface of the fingernail with little effort. See **Photo No. 2-5**. If the bit will not shave a soft fingernail, it certainly will not cut expensive hardwoods efficiently either.

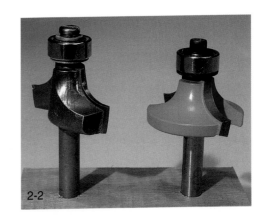

Photo No. 2-2. Conventional bit left compared to the full body, anti-kickback safety bit at the right.

Photo No. 2-3. Coarse grinding marks visible to the naked eye. This is a new, unused bit. The roughness of the shank is another indication of careless workmanship.

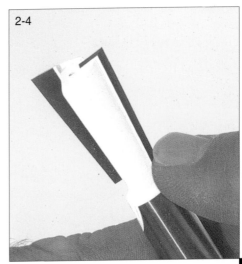

Photo No. 2-4. Lightly sliding the end of a fingernail along the back of the edge will detect rough grinds. *Photo courtesy: Jesada Tools.*

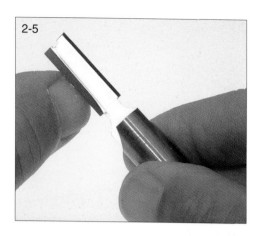

2-5

Engineers can test surface variations of grinding with a profilometer in micro inches (millionth of an inch). A perfectly smooth surface has a "0" rating. Glass and quality ball bearings are around a "2" to "4" rating. Face grinds of Taiwanese bits come in around "40". Some American manufacturers produce bits under "10" and one company expects to reach a "2" rating shortly. Smooth face and bevel grinds accelerate chip ejection so the chips are not being cut again and again. The bit with good chip ejection cuts cooler and its surfaces stay cleaner. Rough grinds attract and increase pitch and gum build-up. This in turn creates heat which sets off chemical reactions at the cutting edge which, as strange as it may sound, accelerates dulling more so than normal abrasive wear.

Chip Formation

Observing the size of chips coming off the bit can tell a lot about the bit and the geometry of the cutter. A bit must be sharp to eject large thin slices of wood that fall to the floor like big snowflakes. See the **Photo No. 2-6**. Saw-dust-like waste indicates too slow of a feed rate, a poorly designed bit, or dull edges.

Photo No. 2-5. Rotate the edge against your fingernail to check for sharpness. *Photo courtesy: Jesada Tools.*

2-6

Photo No. 2-6. Sharp bits produce large, thin, snowflake-like shavings.

Photo No. 2-7. Thin carbide is an indicator of cost cutting.

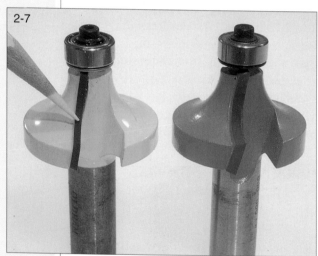

2-7

Photo No. 2-8. Gaps or voids in the brazing could mean big trouble. *Photo courtesy: Jesada Tools.*

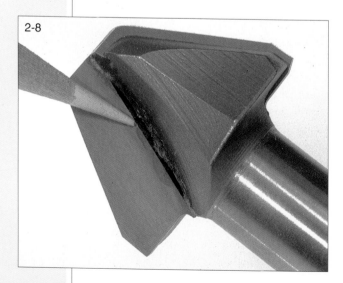

2-8

Carbide Quality

Improved carbides and new grinding technology allows manufacturers to provide much sharper edges than were possible just a few years ago. Carbide grades, however, can vary considerably from manufacturer to manufacturer. Unfortunately, this critical component is very difficult to analyze without special laboratory equipment. There are, however, some ways to avoid inferior carbide.

Grain Structure: Insist on bits with micrograin carbide. Tungsten carbide is actually composed of tiny granules of carbide powder chemically bonded together. The size of the granule is critical to the performance of the bit. Cheap or coarse-grained carbide crumbles quickly, lowering the quality of cut right along with it. Micrograin carbide wears very slowly, stays sharp longer, and less carbide needs to be removed when sharpened.

Carbide Thickness: The amount of carbide, in terms of thickness, is an indicator of quality or it may suggest a manufacturer's desire to cut costs. Less carbide means less edge support and fewer sharpenings, which translates to early replacement. See **Photo No. 2-7**.

Brazing

Check the braze that holds the carbide to the body. If there are any gaps or voids—Beware! See **Photo No. 2-8**. Weak or sloppy brazing may fail at high speed, creating a very dangerous situation. Clean, voidless flutes that don't retard chip ejection are essential.

Shear Angle

Bits with a shear angle or spiral cutting edge slice the wood as they rotate much

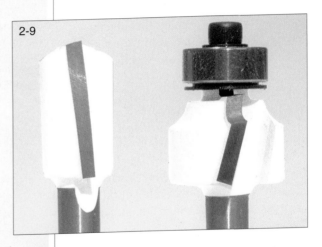

Photo No. 2-9. Bits with shear. Note the cutting edges appear to slant forward or backward in relation to the vertical center axis of the bit. *Photo courtesy: Jesada Tools.*

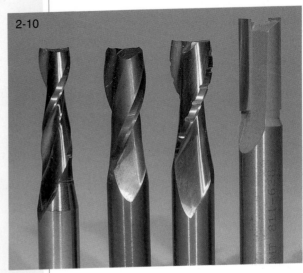

Photo No. 2-10. Spiral bits are better for deep cuts than the straight flute style at the right because they get the chips out more efficiently.

like a knife or plane blade does when it is held at an angle to the work piece. This action produces a smoother edge than bits with straight cutters which tend to chop the wood. See **Photo No. 2-9**.

Making the best choice when buying bits depends upon a combination of many factors: size, cutting shape or profile needed, how it is to be used, and expected life. Experienced router users can do more with fewer bits. Rabbets, for example, can be cut with straight pilotless bits (**Photo No. 2-10**) if used with fences or pin router set-ups. Thus, a single straight bit can also be used to cut dadoes, grooves, finger joints, mortises, and more. Consequently, the router craftsman will purchase a higher quality bit because more is expected of it. The instant a bit is used, it will never be new again, only "like new." That is only if it is a good quality bit that holds its edge and does not require frequent sharpenings because of premature dulling.

Other aspects of selecting and using bits that pertain more directly to safety concerns than bit manufacturing quality are mentioned in **Chapter 4: Router Safety Precautions** on page 25.

Sampling of Bits

Bits are generally designed to either make cuts along an edge or cuts into the flat surface. As noted previously, some bits permit doing both, but bits with bottom ball bearings are intended for edge work only.

Trimming & Pattern Bits

Trimming and pattern bits, **Photos No. 2-11 and 2-12**, are ideal for reproducing duplicate parts. Designed to follow patterns or templates of straight or irregular shapes, bits of this type are among the author's favorites. Turn to pages 50 and 52 which show these in use.

Surface Cutting Bits

Surface cutting bits are used for cutting all sorts of decorative surface embellishments. See **Photos No. 2-13 and 2-14**. These bits may also be used with fences or guides to shape the edges of wood. Bits fitted with shank mounted guide bearings are intended to follow templates or patterns.

Edge Forming Bits

Edge forming bits make cuts that are almost always exposed and visible. Some are much more decorative than others. The simple round-over bit (**Photos No. 2-15 and 2-16**) has been available for a long time. One new innovation just introduced is a carbide tipped version with a small integral pilot. This is perfect for rounding over scroll cut shapes with openings too small for a ball bearing type pilot.

Photo No. 2-11. Trimmer bits are available in all sizes, from ¼" diameter to 1⅛" diameters.

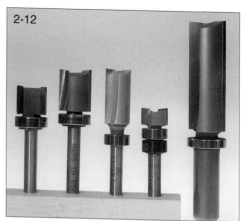

Photo No. 2-12. Pattern bits are essentially straight bits with shank mounted bearings the same size as the cutting diameter.

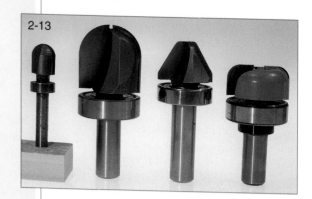

Photo No. 2-13. Some special shape cutters with shank mounted guide bearings.

Photo No. 2-14. A variety of small surface cutting bits.

Photo No. 2-15. Typical carbide round-over with ball bearing pilot at left, and a new carbide tipped bit from Eagle America and MLCS with small diameter (5/32") integral pilot.

Moulding cutters and a few sample bits with decorative cutting profiles are seen in **Photos No. 2-17, 2-18, and 2-19**.

Joint Cutting Bits

There are all kinds of special purpose bits available designed to cut specific joints. Dovetail, biscuits, dado, drawer lock, finger joint, lock miter, mortising, slotting, rail and style, and other single purpose bits. New rabbeting bits have become more versatile. See **Photo No. 2-20**. With as many as seven interchangeable bearings, one bit will cut a variety of rabbets from 1/8" to 1/2" and with the largest bearing that matches the cutting diameter, it becomes a flush trim bit. However, it has only a 1/2" cutting edge length. See **Photo No. 2-21**.

Raised panel bits are also edge cutting. There are two types available, i.e., the vertical and horizontal. See **Photo No. 2-22**. Both styles are intended to be used in the router table. A high fence should always be used with the vertical bit. This bit is obviously safer to use of the two, but it can only be used to cut along straight edges. The horizontal bit

Photo No. 2-16. Rounding over all edges of this fret work would be impossible with a typical 3/8" diameter ball bearing piloted bit.

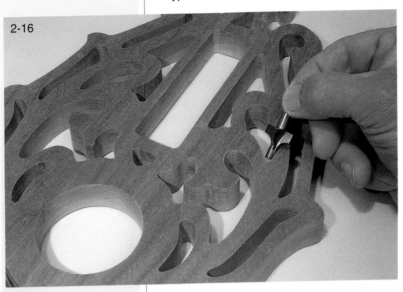

Photo No. 2-17. Bits that cut a variety of decorative edge and molding profiles.

Photo No. 2-18. A typical Ogee at left, and a new triple radius bit at the right that allows for using one, two, or all three radii depending upon the depth of cut.

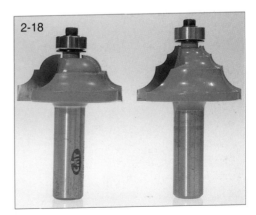

Photo No. 2-19.
A decorative edge cut with an Ogee bit.

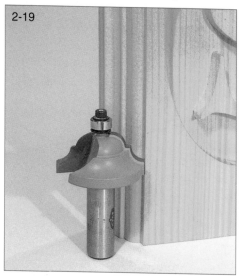

Photo No. 2-21.
Bevel cutting chamfer bits are available in six popular angles. Here a miter joint is cut with the work piece secured to a pattern or straight edge with double faced tape.

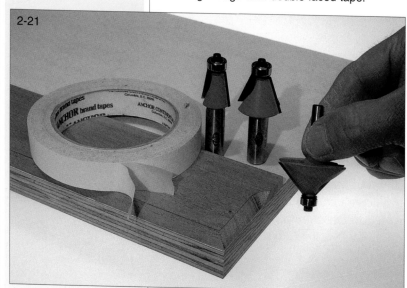

Photo No. 2-20.   With seven interchangeable bearings available, this bit cuts rabbets from ⅛" to ½". One bearing matches the cutting diameter converting it to a flush trim bit.
Photo courtesy: Jesada Tools.

Photo No. 2-22.   Panel raising bits. Vertical type on the left, and horizontal style at the right.

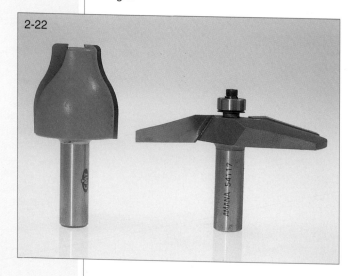

needs to be well guarded. This type has the advantage of following curved edges with its ball bearing pilot.

Other styles and some special bits are randomly illustrated in other chapters.

Care & Sharpening of Bits

It doesn't take long when building a collection of good bits to have invested a substantial amount money. It is obviously prudent to take good care of the collection and take necessary steps to make every bit last as long as possible. Carbide, because it is hard and brittle, probably gets more nicks, chips, and abuse to its cutting edges from careless handling while out of the router than from cutting wood. Keep cutters stored in a covered box or drawer.

Make a storage board with bored holes so the bits will stand vertically and not touch each other. Keep bits clean. Resinous deposits can build up quickly which causes poor chip ejection and heat build up. As the tool gets hotter, tar and pitch harden—compounding the problem. Use commercial tool cleaning products or oven cleaners to remove such build-ups. Dry lubricants reduce pitch accumulation and prevent rusting and pitting.

Even the very best bits dull after extended use. Although some manufacturers do not recommend this practice, the author periodically hones bits for the very same reasons a wood carver or barber frequently stropes or hones their knives and razors. Honing bits yourself keeps the edge sharp and delays regrinding. Grinding is a special business and something not normally done in the home shop. Grinding services usually remove more material

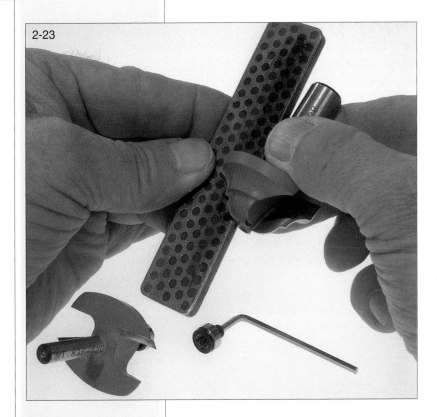

2-23

Photo No. 2-23. Honing an anti-kickback style bit on a diamond stone.

than actually necessary and reduce the long term life of the bit.

A quick do-it-yourself manual honing job is easy. Remove the bearing and always clean to remove pitch, etc. first. Simply place the flat face (chip side) of the bit down on a fine grit diamond stone lubricated with a few drops of water. See **Photo No. 2-23**. The new safety style bits, because of their narrower gullets, must be honed on a thin stone as shown. Larger bench type stones are too thick. Use light pressure and slide the bit back and forth on the stone. Count the number of strokes and make certain to work both surfaces equally, each with the same number. Do not hone the beveled surface behind the cutting edge. Just work the larger flat surface on the chip side of the cutting edge. Test for sharpness as discussed earlier, reattach the bearing, apply dry lubricant and the bits will be ready to get back to work in a few minutes.

Chapter 3: Router Tables

Today every serious woodworking artist knows about or uses a router table of one type or another; if not intimately, at least casually. See **Photos No. 3-1 and 3-2**. Router tables convert the hand-held router to a machine that makes many routing tasks safer, easier, and faster. There are essentially two kinds of router tables: bench-top and floor model. See **Photos No. 3-3 to 3-5**. They can be of either a shop made type or the purchased variety.

It is rather interesting to observe the evolution of router table design. Each year brings a number of new innovations and more sophisticated designs. The author's first router table was simply a piece of plywood supported on saw horses. About four decades and several models later the router table shown in **Photos No. 3-3 and 3-4** seems to satisfy major needs.

Space does not allow for discussion or illustration of all the new concepts in router table designs. A quick overview, however, would reveal router table tops made from heavy cast iron, aluminum (**Photo No. 3-1**), steel plate (**Photo No. 3-2**), and plastic laminate over MDF or other sheet material substrates (**Photos No. 3-3, 3-4, and 3-5**). Router tables can be equipped with high-tech extruded aluminum fences with micro adjustments, imaginative dust collection hook-ups, stops, guards, hold-downs, hold-ins, and about any accessory imagined or desired.

There are router tables with sliding tops that carry the work past the bit. Some router tables have tilting fences or provisions to tilt the router so the bit's axis is not only vertical but adjustable

Photo No. 3-1. This light-duty bench-top Sears router table is one of four models offered by the company. It is designed to hold their Craftsman ¼" collet routers. This model measures 14⅝" high x 13¼" x 34".

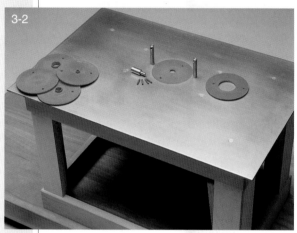

Photo No. 3-2. A heavy-duty bench-top version of the Veritas router table features a ³⁄₁₆" thick x 16" x 24" steel top with a variety of optional accessories available. It is shown with a selection of interchangeable inserts.

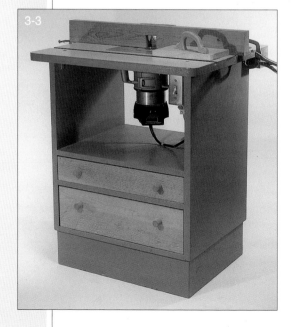

Photo No. 3-3. The author's "ultimate" router table with a simple wooden fence, one of many interchangeable fences made for different categories of work.

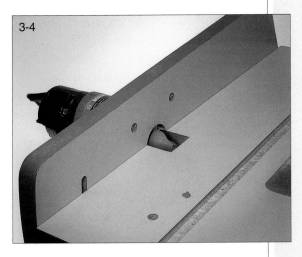

3-4

Photo No. 3-4. This basic accessory holds the router horizontally, with provision for up and down adjustment; it is used for special router joinery. Plans for the author's router table are published in the book *Router Jigs and Techniques*.

3-5

Photo No. 3-5. Join Tech's table design, called the complete "Routing Center." Plans and a "how-to" video are available. This unit has many built-in features including drawers for bits and accessories and an enclosed router compartment with a rear exhaust port to remove dust and chips. Shown with this deluxe "do-it-yourself" cabinet is Join Tech's precision incremental positioning fence.

Photo No. 3-6. This computer-generated graphic illustrates the major features of the Veritas router top and accessories. *Courtesy: Lee Valley.*

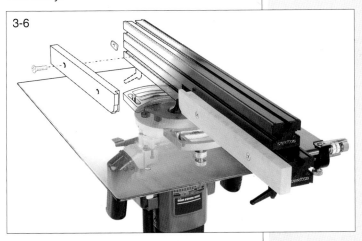

3-6

Photo No. 3-7. Magnets in this Veritas dust chute permit optimum placement for dust collection at the point of cut for most every routing operation with or without the fence.

3-7

to various angles. There are devices available for purchase that will support the router horizontally and/or vertically over the table (over-arm). Accessories can also be found that will attach routers to radial arm saws, drill presses, table saws, and even wood lathes.

The Veritas Router Table Top (**Photos No. 3-2 and 3-6**) has some notable design features. This top can be used with a portable bench top stand and carried to job sites or used in shops where space is a premium. It could also be built into any kind of floor standing unit or cabinet. The fact that it is a ³⁄₁₆" flat steel plate is unusual, and it does offer one distinct advantage in that a magnetized dust collection head (**Photo No. 3-7**) is easily positioned for use behind the fence or anywhere on the table for piloted edge routing.

Once the router clamping mechanism is aligned and the stops are set for a specific router, the router can be installed or removed in just seconds. See **Photo No. 3-8**. This is a real plus for the single router shop.

The Veritas unit has one of the best systems of interchangeable inserts available to keep the opening around the bit safely to a minimum. See **Photos No. 3-1 and 3-9**.

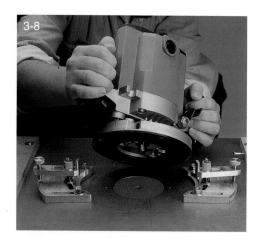

Photo No. 3-8. This flipped-over view shows the underside of the Veritas top and the mechanism that clamps the router securely in position. Usually the sub-base can be left on the router and the system provides quick removal or mounting without wrenches.

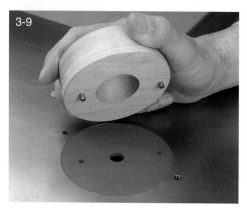

Photo No. 3-9. A wooden "wrench" with two pins engages the plastic insert for a twist, cam action lock that holds it securely in place.

Photo No. 3-10. A split fence provides adjustment to accommodate various size bits.

An extruded aluminum split fence is adjustable lengthwise to accommodate various size bits. See **Photo No. 3-10**. It is also designed so hold-downs, hold-ins, stops, and other accessories can be clamped to it easily because of its T-slotted design. A micro-adjustment accessory is also available.

The Mill-Right Router Table, at first glance, looks like a converted table saw, but it is actually an unusual combination router table/milling center. This machine offers the owner the capability of mounting the router in several ways: with the bit pointing up, down, or horizontally. See **Photos No. 3-11, 3-12, and 3-13**.

The cast iron construction of the Mill-Right includes components that provide work holding positions at

virtually every possible angle to the router bit. The combination of a moveable carriage, hand cranks, and lead screw systems permits moving either the router or the workpiece.

The Mill-Right carriage system also functions as an overhead bridge planer capable of router-surfacing work pieces up to 27" in width. A lathe accessory, when used in conjunction with the router carriage, will produce spindles, tapering, multi-sided turning, and, of course, fluting as well. See **Photo No. 3-14**.

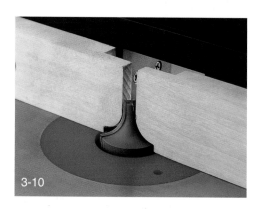

Photo No. 3-11. The Mill-Rite in a typical router table mode with a set-up for box joint machining using a tenoning fixture.

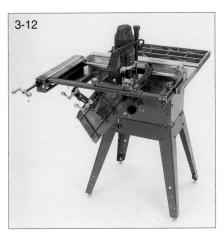

Photo No. 3-12. The Mill-Rite with the router mounted on the carriage above an auxiliary work holding table (below) which is tilted 45° and also 45° about a vertical axis.

Photo No. 3-13. The router in a horizontal position on the carriage to view the blind grooving of the workpiece which was held at 45° and machined for a splined miter.

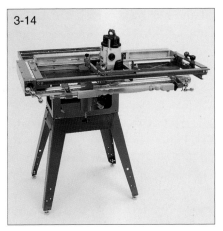

Photo No. 3-14. The router carriage coupled with a lathe accessory mills spindle work which is turned by hand as the router cuts from above.

Chapter 4: Router Safety Precautions

The hazards associated with routing can be substantial if the operator does not approach this work seriously and conscientiously. It is absolutely essential to always be mindful of what the hazards are and then take every precautionary measure to eliminate and minimize the possibility of any mishap.

Think about it! The router is a free-wheeling motor that is hand-held and spins essentially unguarded cutters at extremely high speeds. In use, the portable router is moved about and around the body working a variety of materials and sometimes in crowded conditions. Think about what comes off of the router—from fine dust to knots, chips, and wood splinters or brittle and sharp trimmings from laminates and solid surfacings.

There are hand-held routers that have more than twice the horsepower of some 10" table saws. Saws can be fitted with guards. The fixed-base router can be very dangerous for certain jobs. The unprotected cutter is always extended below the base. Some cuts, like mortising and other surface routing, require lowering the rotating bit into the work while the base is not yet in complete contact with the workpiece. The fixed base router must be tipped to enter the bit while supported only by a portion of the base's edge. Plunge type routers are safer for this sort of work, but, as a rule, do not perform as well when edge routing or are as well suited to certain router table jobs.

Until routers get brakes, the bit continues spinning after the switch is turned off — a disturbing thought, should a bit happen to bend or come loose from the collet.

The router is frightfully loud, not only to the user but to all within hearing distance. In addition to polluting sound waves, the router can contaminate the air by generating hazardous micro dust particles that require good respiratory protection. See **Photos No. 4-1 and 4-2**. Microscopic dust particles, invisible to the naked eye, can linger in the shop for days. Fine airborne dust, generated from working many hardwood exotics, some domestic hardwoods, plastics, and common softwoods such as redwood and cedars, can be extremely harmful. The dust that blankets the workshop is not only unhealthy, it also makes finishing projects more difficult.

Many shop owners are adding auxiliary shop air filtration systems. See **Photo No. 4-2**. These operate quietly and continually filter the shop air as often as several times per hour depending upon shop size, the filter efficiency, fan and motor sizes, and CFM (cubic feet per minute) ratings. An economical alternative for someone who only needs occasional protection is a battery operated respirator/face shield shown in **Photo No. 4-1**. Those have a four-hour battery and only weigh 1¼ pounds.

The only viable approach to router and general shop safety is to always be prepared, mentally and physically. Keep saftey as a primary focus and do not allow any distractions. Use good equipment, know its limitations, and use it only as it was intended to be used. It is extremely dangerous, for example, to operate a hand-held router while holding it upside down. One individual was seriously hurt trying to complete a large bull-nose cut under a counter top's front edge using the router upside down.

Always dress safely; wear tight clothing along with appropriate eye, hearing, and respiratory protection. Know the equipment and read the user's manual. Before starting any routing operation, mentally run through the job, analyzing it from the start through completion.

Ensure that the floor is uncluttered, dry and provides firm, balanced footing. Disconnect the router from the power source when changing bits, attaching accessories, or servicing. See **Photos No. 4-3 and 4-4**.

Insert the bit completely into the collet. Do not use long bits in routers that have poorly designed or short collets.

Photo No. 4-1. Eye, ear, and respiratory protection devices are essential. Note the power visor containing a battery-powered fan which draws in air and filters it before it flows over the face.

Photo No. 4-2. A ceiling mounted air filtration system quietly filters the shop air several times per hour, removing invisible dust particles.

Photo No. 4-3. Disconnect the router from the power source when changing bits or servicing the router.

Photo No. 4-4. Use a foot switch if the switch on the router is difficult to reach or does not operate easily.

Photo No. 4-5. Left: The long bit in this small collet is a mismatch that is likely to cause problems of runout and chatter. Shorter shanks and longer collets make for a much safer combination.

Photo No. 4-5. Inspect collets and bit shanks for any scoring. Replace worn or defective parts immediately.

Feed Direction & Bit Diameter

Always employ the correct feed direction, i.e. against the rotation of the bit. See **Photos No. 4-6, 4-7, and 4-8**. When feeding the router (or moving the workpiece on a router table) correctly, the rotational force of the cutter will pull the bit into the work, making it easy to keep the pilot against the work when doing edge or template routing. If the feed is in the opposite direction, the bit will wander away from its intended path and it will be difficult to control the router or workpiece.

Small diameter bits can bend or break if pushed beyond their limits. The dovetail bit, for example, is one cutter that, by nature of its design, has a definite weak spot. See **Photo No. 4-9**. In use, the dovetail bit is one that actually becomes trapped in its own cut. It cannot be lifted from the work during cutting whereas a straight bit can be lifted from a mortise. With cuts like sliding dovetails, the bit may choke on its own shavings impacted in the cut.

Photo No. 4-6. The correct, safest feed directions when inside and outside edge routing and/or following templates with piloted bits using a hand-held router.

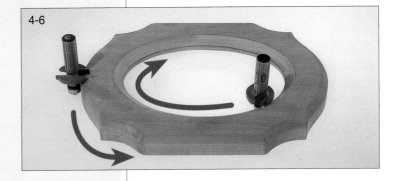

Photo No. 4-7. Safe feed direction for outside edge and template work on the router table.

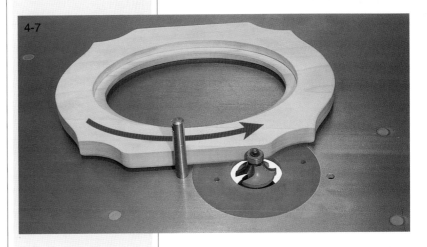

Photo No. 4-8. Safe feed direction for inside edge and template routing on the router table.

To avoid this, pre-cut a dado or groove, as shown in **Photo No. 4-10,** and remove a majority of the waste.

Large diameter cutters (**Photo No. 4-11**) always demand the utmost respect. A woodworker using large diameter cutters rotating at high speeds is definately asking for trouble. These cutters should never be used in small, hand-held, single-speed routers. The rim speed of a bit increases as the diameter increases. A router bit 1½" in diameter rotating at 22,000 R.P.M. has a rim speed of 144 feet per second—about 98 miles per hour. A 3" diameter bit roughly doubles those numbers. When using large diameter cutters, **always** use the router table, reduce the speed, and make successive passes instead of deep cuts. See **Photo No. 4-12**. Below are some R.P.M. guidelines.

Suggested Router Speeds

Bit Diameters	Maximum Speeds (R.P.M.)
1"	24,000
1¼" to 2"	18,000
2¼" to 2½"	16,000
3" to 3½"	10,000 to 12,000

Become familiar with the sound and feel of a properly operating router, both when free running and when cutting under load. Stop immediately at the first sign of any change in sound or feel, especially vibrating sensations. Make deep cuts in multiple passes. Do not use dull bits; keep them clean and sharp.

Photo No. 4-9. Dovetail bits, by the very nature of their design, are structurally weak at this point and consequently must be used carefully and not overloaded.

Photo No. 4-10. Pre-cut a dado or groove to remove excess waste prior to making this type of dovetailed dado cut.

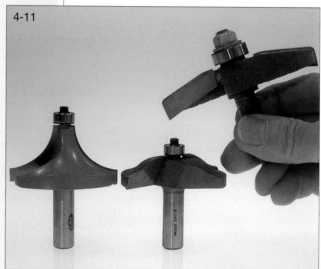

Photo No. 4-11. Large bits such as these can be extremely hazardous if used carelessly.

Photo No. 4-12. This speed control accessory is available to reduce the R.P.M. of single-speed routers. Make certain to check with the manufacturer to assure it will not damage router circuitry.

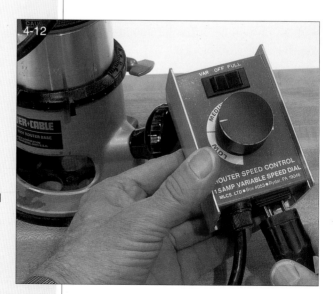

Non-joinery tasks such as routing circles, arcs, or ovals and creating inlays, sign work, and decorative cuts into or through a surface are all typical jobs for the creative router artist. See **Photos No. 5-1 through 5-4** which show some circular routing and some other routing capabilities using a "Pivot Frame Jig" from Trend Routing Technology of England.

The market offers many other types of trammel circular routing guides that have been well illustrated in other books. Trend's new combination ellipse and circle cutting jig shown in the **Photo No. 5-5** is one of a few that are commercially available. One unit will actually cut large elliptical shapes for making table tops.

Sometimes certain jobs dictate that the router artist employ a combination of guided and freehand routing skills. This is especially true when carving incised or raised letters in routed wood sign work. See **Photos No. 5-6 through 5-11**. A variety of templates can be purchased that guide the router to carve anything from incised letters to shapes such as grapes, hearts, or animal profiles.

Photos No. 5-12 and 5-13 illustrate some interesting linear designs created with plastic templates from the Line Art Co. of Emmerson, New Jersey. Templates of this type are intended to be used with a plunge router fitted with a template guide mounted to the router's base. The outside diameter of the template guide matches the slot widths of the plastic template.

A new template-guided surface carving system created and patented in

Photo No. 5-1. Small radius routing with Trend's Pivot Frame Jig produces this array of simple rosettes, radiused designs and circular inlays. *Photo courtesy: Trend Routing Technology.*

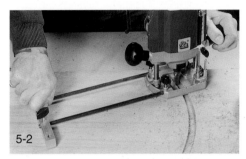

Photo No. 5-2. A typical circular routing jig with a center point and trammel, using components from Trend's Pivot Frame Jig.

Photo No. 5-3. How the "Pivot Frame Jig" cuts small circles, rings, and intricate inlay work without relying on a center point.

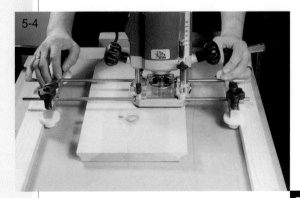

Photo No. 5-4. Set-up for surface planing or routing decorative linear cuts.

Photo No. 5-5. Trend's small version of their "Ellipse and Circle Cutting Jig." The two sliding centers, guided by T-slots, control the router for perfect ovals for picture frames, mirrors, clocks, signs, and table tops.

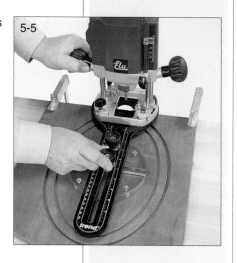

Photo No. 5-6. Freehand routing of irregular curves is often combined with guided straight line cuts in wooden sign work.

Photo No. 5-7. Incised work by Bob Spielman features a masterful combination of straight-edge guided and free-hand cuts.

Photo No. 5-8. A closer look. All the letters were cut with this ¼" upcut spiral bit.

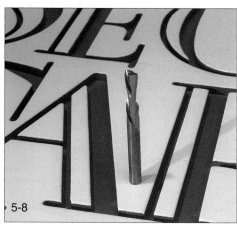

Photo No. 5-9. This very large sign by the author and son, Bob, features 2" high relief letters and incised work.

Photo No. 5-10. A closer look. The background is routed to simulate a hand-carved appearance.

Photo No. 5-11. Freehand routed alphabet by Tom McKree requires much practice and a deft use of the router to create the sweeping serifs and varying depths of cut.

5-11

5-12

Photo No. 5-12. Line Art's templates are made of ½" plastic. A plunge router with a template guide guarantees perfect cuts.

5-13

Photo No. 5-13. Designs in wood and liquid filled inlays in solid surfacing cut with Line Art's templates.

Australia is gathering much acclaim from users in North America and England. See the project **Photos No. 5-15 and 5-16** and refer to pages 63–65 for construction information.

The 3-D surface carving system requires the use of a plunge router with a ½" collet. The idea was originally conceived to produce repeatable carved detailing on the flat surfaces of furniture, entry doors, and the panels of kitchen cabinet doors and drawer fronts. See **Photo No. 5-17**. As one can imagine and visualize, however, this type of guided incised carving can easily be incorporated into many wood projects—large and small.

This carving system consists of three key components:
1. A special 90° V-grooving bit with a ½" shank housed inside an aluminum shaped cone guide. See **Photo No. 5-18 and Drawing 5-18A**.

2. Template(s). More than 50 different designs are available and more are coming. In use, the templates are usually flipped over and/or turned end to end to produce the complete design. Sometimes three individual templates may be required to complete the carving of more complex designs.

3. A Template Holding Frame. This is temporarily secured to the workpiece with double-faced tape or clamps. The holding frame locates the template for routing (**Photo No. 5-19**) and facilitates repositioning when turning and flipping the template for the successive series of router cuts.

The surface carving system is marketed under the name of "3-D Carver" by Jesada Tools of Oldsmar, Florida and their dealers. Jesada Tools has the

North American distribution rights. The same system is also available in England from Trend Machinery and Cutting Tools Ltd.

Photo No. 5-14. This beautiful and functional bathroom heat radiator cover, made of Corian®, has linear designs cut through the surface.

Photo No. 5-15. A clock with router carved surface details produced with an overlapping "Folklore" design corner template.

Photo No. 5-16. Corian® mirror-shelf with template guided surface carving created using just one-half of the "Blaze" design drawer front template.

Photo No. 5-17. Typical surface carving designs on doors and drawers of kitchen cabinetry. *Photo courtesy: Jesada Tools.*

Photo No. 5-18. The three components of the Router Carver System: 1. The bit with aluminum cone housing. 2. A repositionable and interchangeable ¾" thick MDF template, one of many design configurations available. 3. A template holding frame, ½" thick.

Drawing No. 5-18A. The depth of cut is controlled and it automatically changes according to the changing width of the template slot as the bit is moved along.

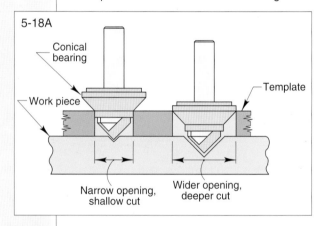

5-18A

Conical bearing

Template

Work piece

Narrow opening, shallow cut

Wider opening, deeper cut

Photo No. 5-19. A plunge router with the V-grooving bit, the template, and template holding frame.

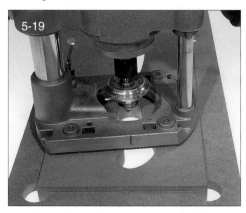

Practically every conceivable joint in woodworking today can be made in its entirety or at least in part using the router. There are numerous joint-making accessories available to guide the hand-held router or control the workpiece on the router table. This chapter provides a quick overview of popular joints along with some of the time-tested accessories and a glimpse of some new devices.

There are a number of self-guiding piloted bits which in themselves are joint-cutting tools. Bits such as the rabbeting bit (**Photo No. 6-1**), slotting cutters used for tongue and grooves, and bits for making biscuit joints are typical examples. Special piloted bits are also available for making lock miters, finger-type glue joints, and the rail and stile joints which are illustrated later.

Panel bits used with special shop-made templates also make rabbet-like cuts and rout recesses for lap joints and hinge mounting. See **Photos No. 6-2 and 6-3**. Straight-line dadoes, rabbets, tongues, and grooves of all sizes are easily made on the router table guided by the fence. See **Photos No. 6-6 and 6-7**.

Box Joints

Box joints are router cut in a variety of ways. Using finger-type templates, such as the Keller or Leigh Jig (**Photo No. 6-8**) with the hand-held router is one way. They can also be cut on the router table as shown in **Photo No. 6-9**. Box joints with eye-catching rounded fingers as cut on the Leigh Jig are relatively new joints. See **Photos No. 6-10 and 6-11A & B**.

Photo No. 6-1. A rabbeting bit cuts this inside rebate to receive an end plug on this box column.

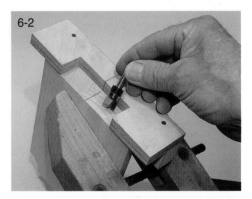

Photo No. 6-2. The shank-mounted bearing on this small panel bit follows a template to cut a shallow rabbeted recess.

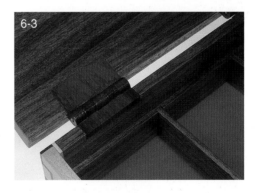

Photo No. 6-3. A wooden hinge fitted into router cut recesses.

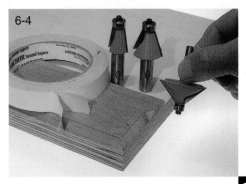

Photo No. 6-4. One method of cutting 45˚ miters or other bevel cuts is to use these piloted chamfer bits.

Photo No. 6-5. Using a piloted chamfer bit to bevel an edge with the hand-held router.

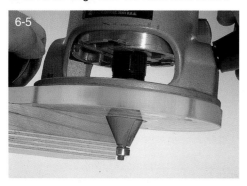

Photo No. 6-6. Very small and precise tongue and groove joinery by Bradford Rockwell is machined on the router table for his mini-boxes.

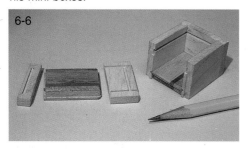

Photo No. 6-7. Rockwell's mini-boxes with sliding lids feature tongue and groove joinery.

Photo No. 6-8. Box joint component as cut on the Leigh Jig with a finger joint template.

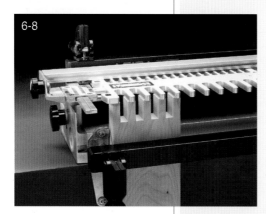

Photo No. 6-9. Cutting box joints on the router table using a jig. It is essentially a "runner strip" the same size as the bit and the spacing between fingers that guides the stacked workpieces as each successive finger is cut. *Photo courtesy: Eagle America.*

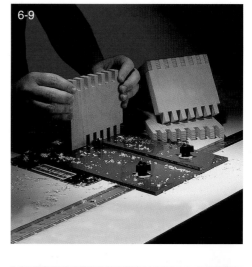

Photo No. 6-10. A "Rounded Half-Blind Finger Joint" created with the Leigh Jig.

Photo No. 6-11A & B. How the components are cut. The router is guided around the template's fingers by a base mounted template guide (guidebush).

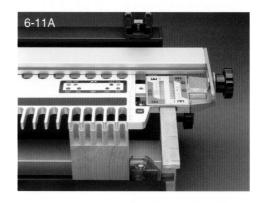

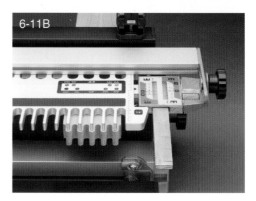

Many joint making accessories, inlay, and template guided work require a template guide (guidebush) mounted to the bottom of the router. The popular Porter-Cable style of template guides, available in many sizes, has been available for a long time. See **Photo No. 6-12**. A new concept, however, comes from Leigh Industries Ltd. in the form of their new "Variable Guidebush System." See **Photos No. 6-12 and 6-13**. The exposed barrel of the bushing has a 5° taper. It is also adjusts up or down, changing the outside diameter of the exposed barrel. Consequently, micro adjustments can be made with the template guide to compensate for slight variations in bit diameters or router bit runout to arrive at the perfect fit.

The Leigh Guidebush is available with adapters to fit any router. This device has good applications where mating pieces are machined during one pass such as when routing certain dovetails and box joint cuts following templates.

Dovetail Joinery

There are several basic kinds of dovetail joints, i.e. half-blind dovetails (**Photos No. 6-14 through 6-17**), through dovetails (**Photos No. 6-18 through 6-23**), and sliding dovetails (**Photo No. 6-24**). There are numerous variations of those joints. Sometimes they are completely concealed in table or carcass work. Sometimes, however, the dovetail work is intentionally made visible so it becomes its own ornamental embellishment.

A wide variety of spectacular box and dovetail right-angle joints that effectively exploit the visual advantages of contrasting wood and precision routing techniques create

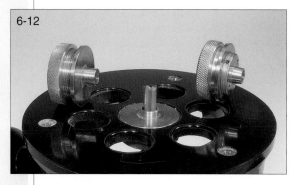

Photo No. 6-12. Conventional uniform diameter template guides in brass and one of the new 5° tapered style guidebush in aluminum from Leigh Industries Ltd.

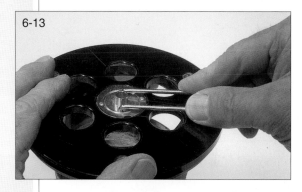

Photo No. 6-13. This wire wrench adjusts the new guidebush up or down which changes the exposed outside diameter slightly to compensate for minor variations in bit diameters and router run-out.

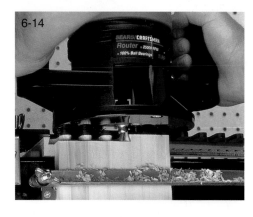

Photo No. 6-14. Half-blind dovetailing with economical fixturing. Both components of the joint are clamped in the jig and cut at the same time.

Photo No. 6-15. Half-blind dovetails cut on the Leigh Jig.

Photo No. 6-16.   Routing the pins for half-blind dovetails on the Leigh Jig. Each component of the joint is cut separately.

Photo No. 6-17.   A different set-up cuts the sockets.

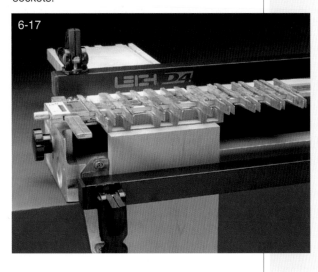

Photo No. 6-18.   Some through dovetail joints and sliding dovetailed lids on routed boxes.

Photo No. 6-19.   Keller's popular ½" thick aluminum dovetail templates come in sets, one each for routing the tails and pins. They have been used by woodworkers for almost two decades.

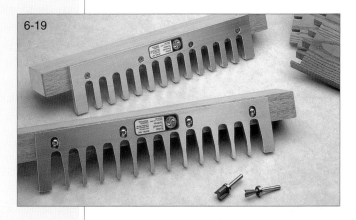

Photo No. 6-20.   Bits with shank-mounted bearings, not template guides, follow the Keller dovetail templates.

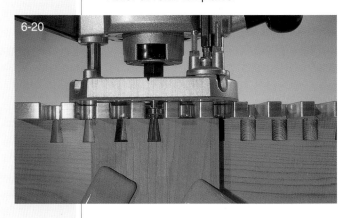

Photo No. 6-21.   New from Keller and Co. is their economical single-piece unit "Journeyman," 15" template with combined back-to-back dovetail and pin template.

Photo No. 6-22. Porter-Cable's "Dovetail Machine" has a cast aluminum base with steel clamps and features a variety of interchangeable templates available that will cut most kinds and sizes of dovetails.

Photo No. 6-23. Variable spaced dovetails can be produced on the Leigh Jig because of the template's adjustable style fingers. *Photo courtesy: Leigh Industries Ltd.*

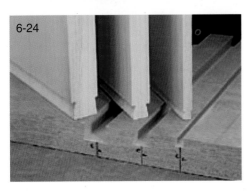

Photo No. 6-24. Sliding dovetails are used for shelving and partitions in carcass construction and sometimes for drawer front to side joints, too. *Photo courtesy: Leigh Industries Ltd.*

some dazzling projects. See **Photos No. 6-25 through 6-28**. This class of work is exclusively a router table activity. Precision fences, i.e. Join-Tech's Incremental Positioner and the Incra Positioning Jig (**Photo No. 6-28**) are router table accessories that make this incredibly exacting joinery work possible.

Pin & Cove

The pin and cove (**Photos No. 6-29 and 6-30**) is another decorative right-angle joint that actually dates to the nineteenth century. See **Photos No. 6-27 through 6-41**. Used on the finest cabinetry of the past century, this joint is currently gaining popularity as an alternative to dovetails on today's finest handmade furniture. The authentic early joints had every pin machined individually as an integral projecting part of the member with the female scallops. The technique involved to make the contemporary version of this joint combines template routing, scroll saw work, and plunge-cut or drilled holes for inserting separate pieces of doweling. **Photos No. 6-32 to 6-41** illustrate the use of the "Spielman Pin and Cove Template," and the essential techniques involved to make this strong and eye-catching joint.

Mortise & Tenon Joints

Like sliding dovetails and other joints, mortise and tenon joints are usually non-exposed, and more functional than decorative. See **Photos No. 6-42 and 6-43**. However, some router artists do find ways to expose the joints to show off their skills and validate their high-quality workmanship. Used primarily for leg and rail construction in tables, chairs, stools, and frames, the mortise and tenon is also found in case and carcass work. See the exposed dove-

Photo No. 6-25. A double, double box joint.

Photo No. 6-26. A double, double dovetail joint.

Photo No. 6-27. Another version of the double, double dovetail joint created by Perry McDaniel with the Incra Jig.

Photo No. 6-28. The Incra Jig in use creating a decorative dovetail joint.

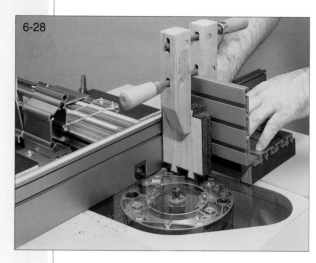

Photo No. 6-29. The elegant pin and cove joint.

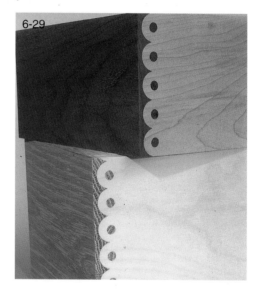

Photo No. 6-30. The Spielman Pin and Cove Template guides the cuts for the female component using a small pattern bit.

Photo No. 6-31. The components of the pin and cove joint. The matching male scallops of the piece on the right are cut with the scroll saw.

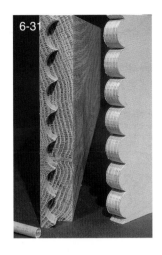

Photo No. 6-32. Centering the template over the end of the workpiece.

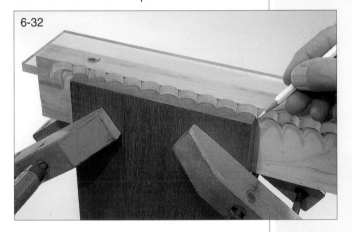

Photo No. 6-33. The routing operation.

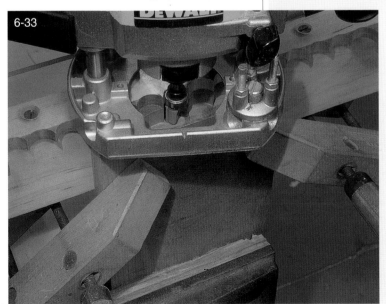

Photo No. 6-34. The template is used as a layout tool to mark the male scalloped cuts for scroll sawing.

Photo No. 6-35. Scroll sawing the male scallops. Note the relief cuts.

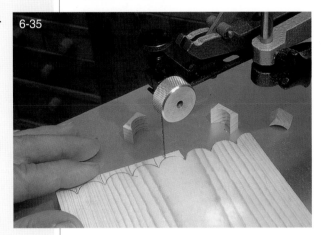

Photo No. 6-36. The initial assembly is made without the dowel pins.

Photo No. 6-37. Devices used for plunge cutting the dowel pin holes. Left: ¼" up-cut spiral bit; Center: ¾" O.D. template guide set unaltered; Right: Optional ¾" O.D. template guide with shortened barrel; Rear: Plywood shim to attach to router base which also effectively shortens the length of the template guide.

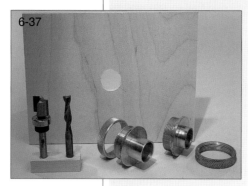

Photo No. 6-38. Using an auxiliary plywood base (shim), attached with double-faced tape, has the same effect as cutting the barrel of a template guide shorter.

Photo No. 6-39. The template is again repositioned over the glued joint and used as a guide for plunge cutting the ¼ inch dowel holes. The ¾" O.D. template guide automatically positions the router for each plunge cut dowel hole.

Photo No. 6-40. Dowels prepared with pre-drawn lines referencing the grain direction.

Photo No. 6-41. A close-up look. Note how the grain direction of the oak pins closely matches the end grain of the oak member, simulating pins machined as if a part of the whole member.

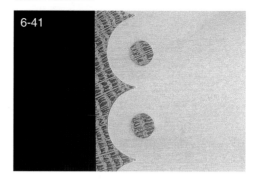

tail mortise and tenon joints on Kim Taylor's Angling West Tables on page 118 and note the wedged through mortise and tenon joints on Jeff Greenup's Bookshelf (**Photo No. 6-44**) on page 79 produced with the Leigh Jig.

Coped Rail & Stile

Coped rail and stile and raised panel work go pretty much hand-in-hand to create cabinetry doors. See **Photos No. 6-45 and 6-46**. New cutters have evolved that make this class of work easier than ever. Improvements to the single bit which required reversing or flipping the cutter on an arbor when switching between stile and rail cuts include using a pair of bits, i.e. one for the stile and another for the rail.

Now a single combination bit is available that allows for making both the rail and the stile cuts without changing bits. See **Photos No. 6-47, 6-48, and 6-49**. Simply raise or lower the bit to switch between rail or stile cutting modes. Reversible and combination type rail and stile bits come with shims to adjust joint tightness and fine tune the bit after sharpening.

Raised Panel Work

Raised panel work is best done on the router table. Remember to slow speeds and take successive passes at shallow cuts when using large diameter bits. Raising panels using the vertical-type bits with the work guided against a high fence is the safest option. See **Photo No. 6-50**.

Photo No. 6-42. Repeated mortising and grooving jobs with the hand-held router, on stock of the same size, is easier if two edge guides are used.

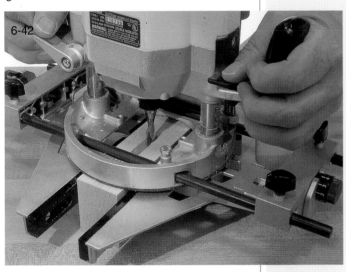

Photo No. 6-43. Typical tenoning jobs are easiest on the router table, either in a set-up with the bit pointing up, or horizontally as shown.

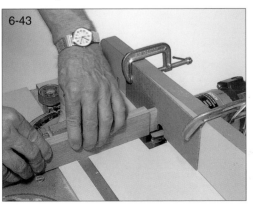

Photo No. 6-44. This series of wedged through mortise and tenon joints of Jeff Greenup's Bookshelf are not only extremely strong but decorative as well. See the project photo and plans on page 79.

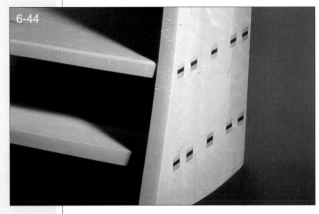

Photo No. 6-45. Samples of coped rail-and-stile frames and raised panel door construction. *Photo courtesy: Trend Machinery and Cutting Tools Ltd.*

Photo No. 6-46. Close-up of typical door section and the bits used. Left: Reversible type of rail and stile bit consisting of cutters and bearing assembled on an arbor. The cutters are rearranged to switch the bit from the rail or the stile-cutting mode to the other. Right: Raised panel bit. *Photo courtesy: Trend Machinery and Cutting Tools Ltd.*

Photo No. 6-47. This combination rail and stile cutter with three cutters and two bearings on one arbor permits switching between rail and stile machining modes without changing bits or moving the fence. *Photo courtesy: Jesada Tools.*

6-47

Photo No. 6-48. Rails are cut with the upper end of the bit. *Photo courtesy: Jesada Tools.*

6-48

Photo No. 6-49. Stiles are cut with the lower portion of the bit. *Photo courtesy: Jesada Tools.*

6-49

Photo No. 6-50. Vertical raised panel work on the router table. *Photo courtesy: Join-Tech.*

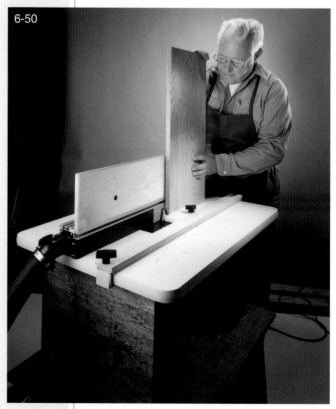

6-50

The router, when used with various accessories, can be an incredible wood forming instrument. The router will, for example, produce a round wood cylinder, then flute it lengthwise or cut decorative beads and flutes around it. A woodworker can also router-cut functional wood threads on dowels, make turnings with multi-sided flats or create turnings with a variety of ornamental, rope-like twists. Three-dimensional carvings can even be duplicated from a master pattern with the router. This chapter provides a brief overview of these fascinating possibilities.

Router Cut Doweling

It is easy to transform square stock into reasonably true, round dowels with just four passes over a round-over bit in the router table. See **Photos No. 7-1 and 7-2**. To produce perfectly round, true-to-size dowels requires high quality tooling and an accurate set-up. Less than perfect dowels are often acceptable for many woodworking projects. Dowels can be made from scrap edgings which is far more economical than buying them ready made. Special jigs and other devices for making round dowels can be found in the author's book, *The New Router Handbook*.

Dowels & Decorative Ends

Dowels with decorative ends are easy to make with the router table and edge-forming bits with ball bearing pilots. See **Photo No. 7-3**. A simple support fence clamped to the router table is all that is necessary to guide the dowel into the bit. By varying the bit height, different profiles can be cut with just one bit.

Photo No. 7-1. Feather boards clamped to the router table are necessary to provide constant pressure when making dowel stock.

Photo No. 7-2. A close-up look at the dowel-making set-up.

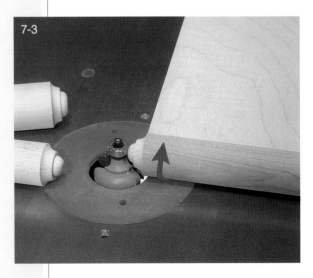

Photo No. 7-3. Making decorative end cuts on dowels. Note the rotational feed direction.

Beall Wood Threading Kits have been available since 1982. See **Photos No. 7-4 and 7-5**. Through the years they have been periodically upgraded. Today, Beall Tooling is available to cut both right- and left-handed threads in these sizes: ½", ⅝", ¾", 1" and, most recently, 1¼" and 1½". Beall also offers a book, *The Nuts and Bolts of Woodworking* which features about 20 unique wood threading projects. See the adjustable wood threaded stool by J. R. Beall on page 70.

Router Lathe

The "Router Lathe" (**Photo No. 7-6**) is a light-duty accessory, yet it is capable of creating a variety of ornamentally turned designs. See the **Photos No. 7-7 and 7-8**. This device is available from Sears in the U.S. and from Trend Machinery and Cutting Tools in England.

The Router Lathe consists of a head stock with an indexing mechanism, a tail stock, and four tubes upon which travels the cable-driven router carriage. Different designs are created by combining five basic types of routing cuts: lengthwise straight beads and flutes; roping or spiral cuts in left and/or right directions; turned beads, coves, etc. cut around the turning; and template-controlled profile turnings.

Phantom's Ornamental Milling System

This is also a lathe-like piece of equipment that carries a router. Phantom's machine is much larger and more durable than the Sears' Router Lathe. It not only has considerably more stock size capacity, it also offers the user a far broader range of exciting

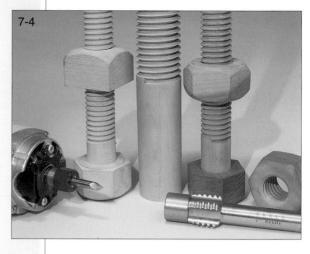

Photo No. 7-4. The Beall wood threading system cuts external threads with a solid carbide bit, left; and internal threads with a tap, right. The taps have removable pilots so they can also serve as bottoming taps.

Photo No. 7-5. Set-up for cutting threads on doweling requires only a light-duty router or trim router as shown.

Photo No. 7-6. Spiral turning on the Router Lathe. *Photo courtesy: Trend Machinery and Cutting Tools Ltd.*

Photo No. 7-7. Hollow spiral turnings and a profile produced with a template guided router. *Photo courtesy: Trend Machinery and Cutting Tools Ltd.*

Photo No. 7-8. A variety of router-produced decorative furniture legs featuring bends, flutes, and diamond patterned surfaces.

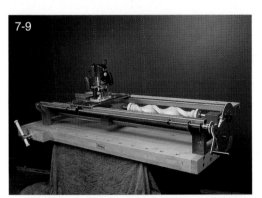

Photo No. 7-9. The bench model, No. 1000 Legacy Ornamental Router Milling Machine. Notice the hand crank operated linear drive screw which moves the router lengthwise in its X-axis as the workpiece, held between centers, slowly rotates.

Photo No. 7-10. Examples of similar template-produced profiles, cut on the Legacy Milling Machine, with various decorative options described left to right: 8 equal sided, 10 spiraled flats, typical round lathe-like work, 8 unequal sides, and ribbon twist.

capabilities. See the **Photos No. 7-9 and 7-10**.

Phantom's machines might be described as an X-Y axis router-controlled milling machine configurated on top of a long lathe. Phantom Engineering recently replaced their "Woodchuck" model, introduced in 1990, with two upgraded 60" length capacity machines called the "Legacy." Available in two models, the 1000 and the 1500, both are essentially the same units except that the model 1500 comes with all of the optional accessories.

When used with the floor stand accessory the maximum diameter capacity increases from 7½" to 9½". The deluxe 1500 model also features a motorized lead screw feed and limit switches that control the direction, distance and speed of the router travel along its X (linear) axis. The router sits in a carrier tray that provides a cross or Y-axis feed direction. The router can be engaged to a hand-screw feed, locked in at any position, or allowed to slide freely with just hand control.

The Legacy is best equipped with a large, heavy-duty plunge router to exploit the full potential of the machine. The router always moves horizontally. The "lathe" bed, with the head stock and tail stock, is raised to mill small diameter projects, like small writing pens, or the bed can be lowered to mill large stock. Either end can be raised or lowered to make tapered milling cuts.

The head and tail stock have typical lathe-like features with Morse taper hollow spindles and an external thread to accommodate a three-jaw chuck and other common lathe accessories as desired. The workpieces can be locked in and indexed to facilitate routing multi-sided shapes and turnings. See the **Photos No. 7-11, 7-12, and 7-13**. In fact, complete Queen Anne style table legs (**Photo No. 7-14**) can be machined. The router follows shop-made templates to cut the various flat profiles and round curved surfaces. A roller stylus on the router base follows the edge of the template (**Photo No. 7-12**) reproducing the profile cut on the workpiece.

The router can be positioned so the bit will enter the workpiece directly from the top or approach it inward from the side.

The spiral drive system is a function of the lineal lead screw and an arrangement of gears that provides a wide choice of different pitches. The choice of pitches ranges from a tight ¾" movement per revolution to a stretched-out 15" per rotation. The drive motor simultaneously moves the router via the lead screw and also rotates the stock. See the sample cuts shown in the **Photos No. 7-15 and 7-17**.

It is impossible to illustrate or describe all of the different styles of cuts and endless combinations of unusual designs that can be generated with this equipment. See **Photos No. 7-16 and 7-18**. Phantom Engineering, Inc. offers a series of educational videos to help the operator understand and use this remarkable machine to its fullest potential. Additional topics include joinery, producing architectural mouldings and mill work, surface routing of flat stock or duplicating plain, old round turnings which, among many other uses, can be done in either a decorative or functional manner.

Photo No. 7-11. Left is the spring-loaded pin which engages into one of the holes of the indexing plate to keep the stock from rotating as it is milled. Also shown is the hexagon spindle work mounting plate called the "Index Drive Center." *Photo courtesy: Phantom Engineering, Inc.*

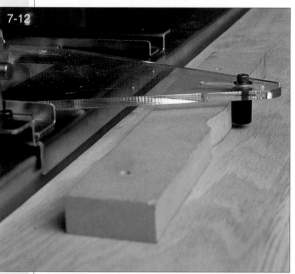

Photo No 7-12. A roller stylus guides the path of the router as it follows this shop-made template to mill a specific profile. *Photo courtesy: Phantom Engineering, Inc.*

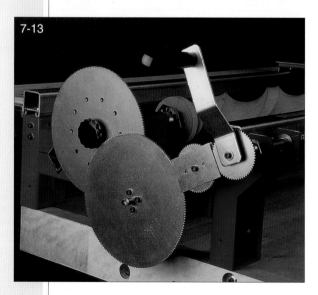

Photo No. 7-13. A view of the hand crank used to drive the lead screw feed, the gear drive system, and the wood template base (shelf) partially visible to the rear right. *Photo courtesy: Phantom Engineering, Inc.*

Photo No. 7-14. A Queen Anne style table leg created by template profile routing on the Legacy Ornamental Mill.

Photo No. 7-16. Canes produced by Monty Gould feature hollow twists and diamond designs. See page 127.

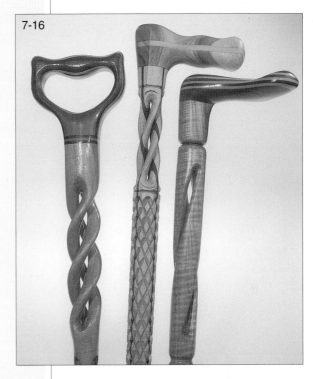

Photo No. 7-17. More spectacular work samples produced with the Legacy Ornamental Mill.

Photo No. 7-15. A variety of cuts and the bits used.

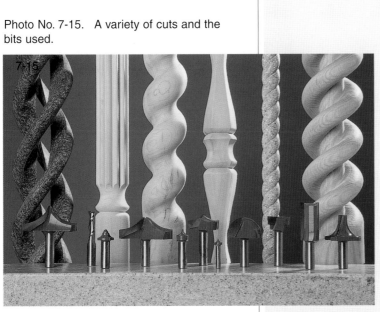

Photo No. 7-18. Router-cut hollow twisted candle holder also by Monty Gould.

machines are, by and large, limited to producing low relief carvings with flat backs and carved wood signs.

Photo No. 7-19. The Dupli-Carver in use creating a 3-dimensional reproduction. The operator moves the stylus over the master pattern, on the right, which repeats the same router cut in the wood at the left.

Router Carving Machines

Router carving machines copy a master pattern or template to carve anything from wood signs to a full 3-dimensional wood bust. See **Photos No. 7-19, 7-20, and 7-21**. The "Dupli-Carver" machines distributed by Terrco of Watertown, South Dakota, uses a small router motor for the carving head. Most carving machines operate somewhat like a pantograph which synchronizes the movement of the stylus and the cutting bit. The Dupli-Carver has a wide range of similar but additional mechanical movements in which the stylus and router move in unison: back and forth, sliding along the horizontal shaft; an up and down plus a rotational motion of the shaft; and in and out achieved pivoting the lower arm.

The Dupli-Carver will copy pieces up to 14" in diameter by 40" in height. Other pantograph type carving

Photo No. 7-20. Duplicating a flat-back carving of a mahogany switch plate from a cast brass pattern.

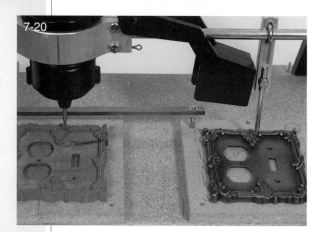

Photo No. 7-21. A 3-dimensional statuary produced with the Dupli-Carver machine.

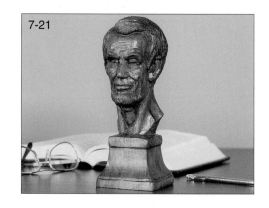

photo by Kevin Dilley for Hazen Photography

Patrick Spielman's Multiple Picture Frame,
butternut,
¾" x 15¾" x 12¾"

Multiple Picture Frame

The solid wood photo frame can be hung vertically, as shown, or horizontally. This is another template routing project. Once the template/pattern is made any number of identically shaped frames can be produced. Apply the very same techniques to make other singular oval and rectangular photo frame configurations from solid wood.

Construction:
The template for this project was made from ⅜" thick Baltic birch plywood, but thinner material will also work.

1. Trace around the template to provide rough cutting guidelines. See **Photo No. 1**.

2. Drill holes as necessary to facilitate sawing out the inside openings. Make rough cuts about ¹⁄₁₆ to ⅛" inside the layout lines.

3. Nail the template to the back of the work as shown in **Photo No. 2**.

4. Rout the openings to finished size and shape on the router table using a flush trim bit, as shown in **Photos No. 3 and 4**. Be sure to always feed against the bit's rotation.

5. Cut ¼" rabbets ⅜" deep around the back inside of each opening.

6. Round-over the edges to a ¼" radius, sand-finish as desired, and attach metal hangers—one for vertical and one for horizontal hanging.

Multiple Picture Frame diagram

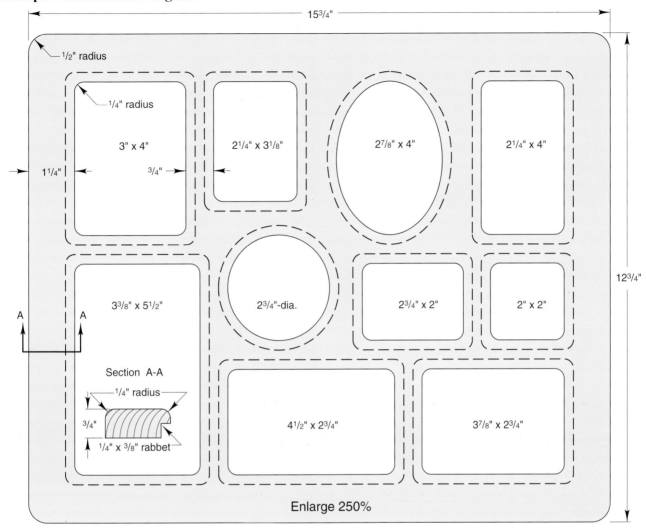

15³/₄"

¹/₂" radius

¹/₄" radius

3" x 4"

2¹/₄" x 3¹/₈"

2⁷/₈" x 4"

2¹/₄" x 4"

1¹/₄"

³/₄"

3³/₈" x 5¹/₂"

2³/₄"-dia.

2³/₄" x 2"

2" x 2"

A — A

Section A-A

¹/₄" radius

³/₄"

¹/₄" x ³/₈" rabbet

4¹/₂" x 2³/₄"

3⁷/₈" x 2³/₄"

12³/₄"

Enlarge 250%

Patina Lamp

This project employs some basic router mass production techniques. Any number of different types of material can be considered for making this lamp. MDF was used because it is inexpensive, machines easily, and can be finished in a variety of ways, even to simulate the popular patina finish that looks like aged metal. Other materials can also be used, such as: plywoods, solid wood, or solid surface (Corian®, Environ®, and others).

Construction:
The general steps of procedure involved to make and finish the metallic lamp shown in **Photo No. 1** is given in the captioned **Photos No. 2 through 14**.

1

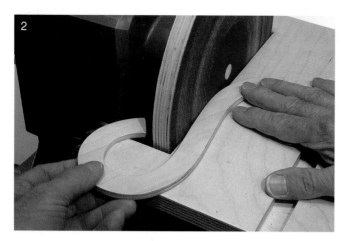

Photo No. 2. First, make a ¼" plywood template. Fair the curves with abrasive and files as necessary.

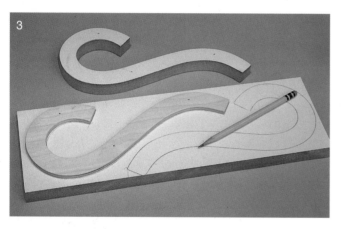

Photo No. 3. Use the template as a pattern and nest the layout for rough cutting to save stock. (Pre-primed MDF was used only to enhance photo clarity.)

Photo No. 4. Rough cut the pieces about 1/16" oversize all around with the band or scroll saw.

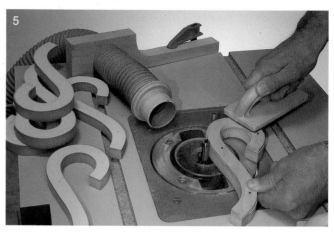

Photo No. 5. Nail the template to each workpiece and trim-cut, making duplicate parts using a trimming bit in the router table.

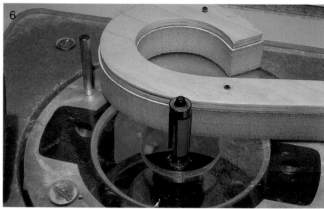

Photo No. 6. A close-up look at the cutting action. Note that the feed is always against the rotation of the bit.

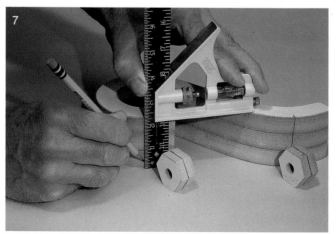

Photo No. 7. Make assembly reference lines on the "S" shaped legs and around the horizontal centers of the center blocks as shown. Soften all sharp edges with sandpaper.

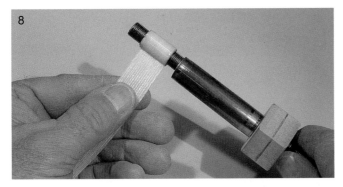

Photo No. 8. Cut the ⅛" continuous threaded pipe and rigid copper tubing to length. Use a tubing cutter to assure that the tubing is cut square. Wrapping tape around the inside pipe at four locations will center it inside this larger tubing.

Photo No. 9. Assembly. Align the "flats" of the center blocks and tighten the assembly with the threaded pipe. Assure that the two pieces of copper tubing align with each other in a continuous straight line. Glue the first leg with gap filling instant glue or epoxy.

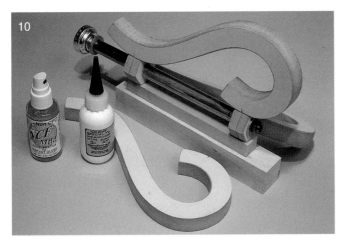

Photo No. 10. Prop up the partial assembly on blocks as shown, and glue on the second leg, then the third leg in the same manner.

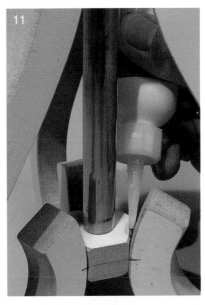

Photo No. 11. Applying a heavy bead of gap filling instant glue to simulate a weld adds to the realistic metal look.

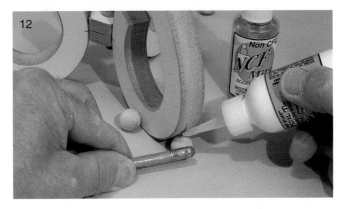

Photo No. 12. Adding wood balls for a little more stability is optional.

Photo No. 13. Applying the first coat of a water based liquid copper (a blend of acrylic and metallic solids) finish. A sponge applied patina solution is applied to a second metallic coating while it is still fresh and uncured.

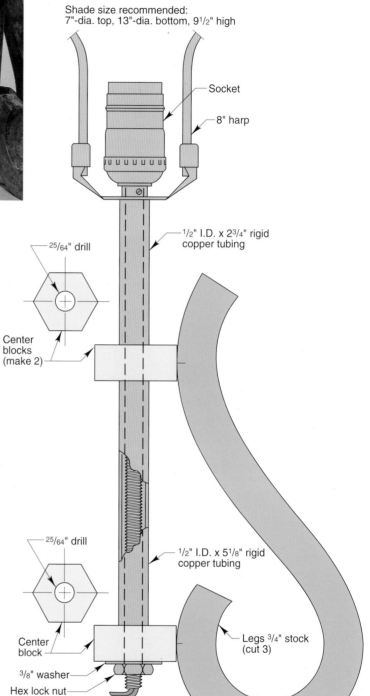

Photo No. 14. The results of the sponge applied patinas: green at left and blue at right.

Patina Lamp diagram

Shade size recommended:
7"-dia. top, 13"-dia. bottom, 9½" high

Socket

8" harp

½" I.D. x 2¾" rigid copper tubing

25/64" drill

Center blocks (make 2)

½" I.D. x 5⅛" rigid copper tubing

25/64" drill

Center block

Legs ¾" stock (cut 3)

⅜" washer

Hex lock nut

7' lamp cord

Enlarge 200%

*Patrick Spielman's Patina Lamp,
MDF, 10" W x 13" H*

Patrick Spielman's Tree Tray,
ash,
¾" x 8½" x 13"

Routed Trays

Basic template routing using dishing or tray cutting bits enables the router artist to create a wide variety of tray, dish, platter, and shallow box-like projects. See **Photos No. 1 and No. 2** on page 56. These bits cut an inside radius, make a flat bottoming cut and a straight vertical wall all at once. This work could also be done using two different cutters: a core box bit or round nose bit to cut the rounded inside corner and the vertical wall and a straight cutting bit to remove the flat inside areas.

Tree Tray Construction:
1. Guide the bit along the template, using a router

base mounted template guide bushing or using bits with shank mounted bearings shown in **Photo No. 2**. Use thicker templates with bearing guided cutters and thinner template stock for guide bushing work. Template thickness relates directly to minimal and maximum depth of cut adjustments.

2. When making pieces with very wide or large recessed openings, equip the router with a larger base, one that bridges across the entire routing area. See **Photos No. 1, 3, and 5**.

The Dust Pan shown in **Photos No. 4 and 5** is interesting in that, except for the pierced scroll saw work, the entire project can be shaped with the router.

Dust Pan Construction:
1. Make the template as shown **Photos No. 5 and 6**. Enlarge and apply the pattern to the work with a temporary bonding adhesive. Rough-cut the outside profile (**Photo No. 7**). Nail the template over the pattern and trim the profile to size in the router table as shown in **Photo No. 8**.

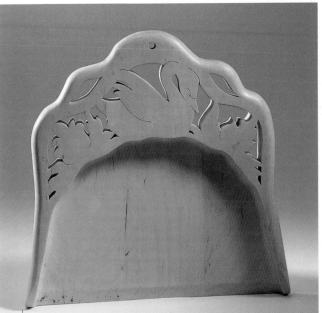

Patrick Spielman's Dust Pan,
maple,
1" x 10" x 9⅝"

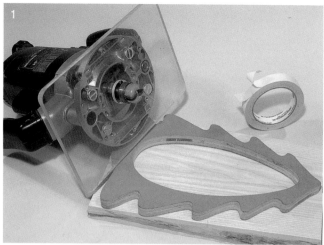

Photo No. 2. Ball bearing guided dishing cutters.

Photo No. 1. The essentials of dish, tray, or shallow box routing. The plywood template is secured to the work piece with double face tape and the router is equipped with an extended or larger base that bridges the template opening.

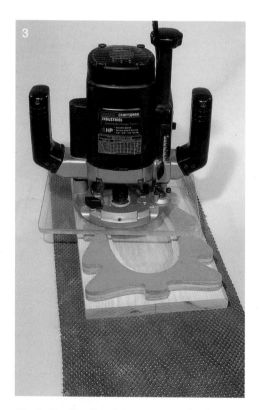

Photo No. 3. Routing on a non-slip pad eliminates the need for mechanical clamping devices that would obstruct router movement.

Tree Tray diagram

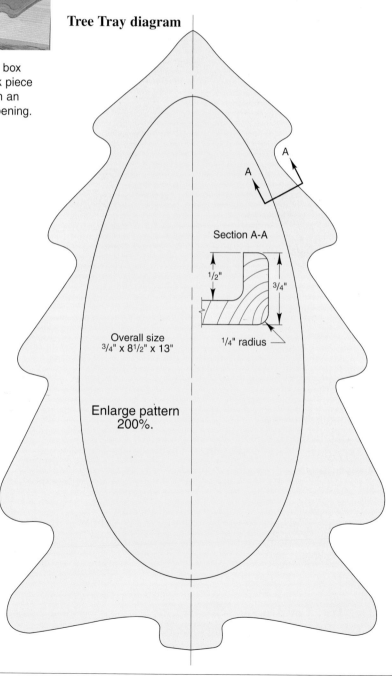

Section A-A

1/2"

3/4"

1/4" radius

Overall size
3/4" x 8 1/2" x 13"

Enlarge pattern
200%.

2. Dish-out the recess and sand. See **Photos No. 9 and No. 10**. Make the fretwork cuts on the scroll saw and remove the pattern. The two 22½° bevels on each surface at the front edge can be cut on the router table while the work is clamped vertically to a wide supporting board. See **Photos No. 11 and No. 12**.

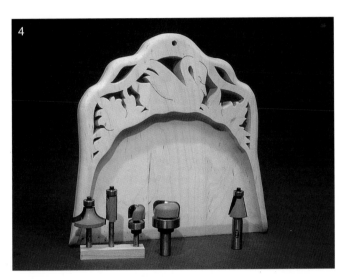

Photo No. 4.   Making this wooden dust pan project involves the same routing principles.

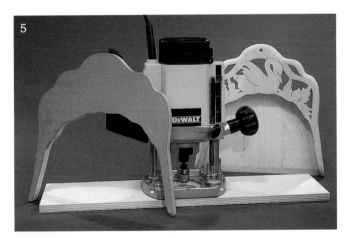

Photo No. 5.   A ¾" MDO plywood template and the router equipped with an extended plywood base.

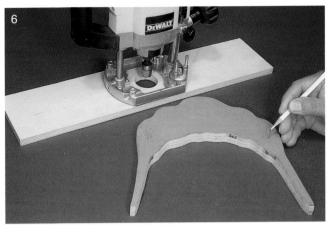

Photo No. 6.   Two finishing nails driven into the waste area of the project will secure the template.

Photo No. 7.   The outside profile cut to rough size and the template nailed over the paper pattern.

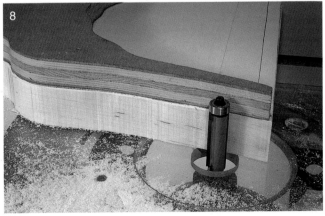

Photo No. 8.   Trimming to size on the router table.

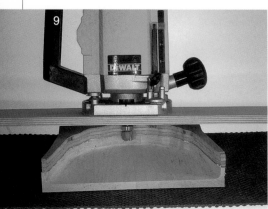

Photo No. 9. Routing the recess on a non-slip bench pad.

Dust Pan diagram

Overall size
1" x 10" x 9⅝"

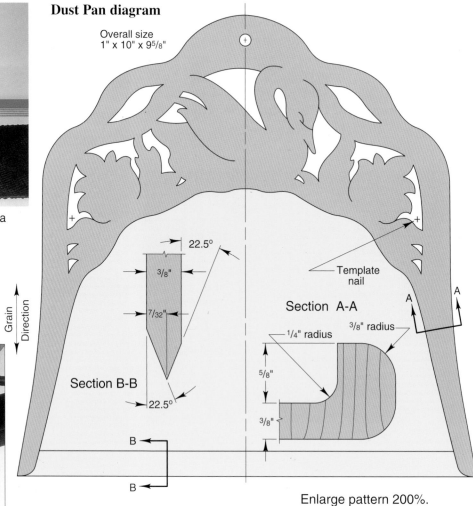

Grain Direction

22.5°

³/₈"

⁷/₃₂"

Section B-B

22.5°

Template nail

Section A-A

¼" radius

³/₈" radius

⁵/₈"

³/₈"

B

B

Enlarge pattern 200%.

Photo No. 10. Sanding.

Photo No. 11. Forming the inside beveled edge on the router table with a 22½° chamfer bit.

Photo No. 12. Routing the back bevel.

*Patrick Spielman's Potpourri Box,
walnut,
4⅝" x 2⅛" H*

Potpourri Box

Some of the routing techniques involved to make this box are similar to those used by other artisan box makers featured later in this book. Though called a potpourri box, it can be used to hold a variety of items and small treasures.

Construction:
1. One template of ¼" x 4⅝" square plywood is used to rout the recessed openings into the bottom and lid. See **Potpourri Box #1 diagram** on page 60 and **Photo No. 1** on page 62. Prepare the box and lid material to their respective 1½" and ¾" thicknesses and cut each 4⅝" perfectly square. Tip-cut the template material, the box, the lid, and an extra piece of ¾" scrap (or two) all to 4⅝" square at the same time on the table saw. Do not cut to the octagon shapes until later.

2. The template is secured to the work for routing with nails driven into the waste corners. It is helpful, and maybe faster, to rough out the inside material using a Forstner bit giving the router a lighter work load. See **Photo No. 2**. Rout both pieces to full depth using the same template. Assure that the nail heads are set below the surface. See **Photos No. 3 and 4**.

3. Carefully make the necessary plywood work holding jig for the table saw. See **Potpourri Box #1 diagram** and **Photo No. 5**. Saw the opening, saving a fine layout line. File to final fit. Use one of the extra 4⅝" squared pieces of ¾" scrap for a test run. Check to assure that the saw fence is positioned correctly so the angular cuts will result in a perfectly true octagon with all eight surfaces absolutely equal.

4. Rabbet the inside edge of the box all around. See the section view on the drawing. If using a rabbeting bit with interchangeable bearings, it is unlikely that a rabbet can be created that is 5⁄32" wide as specified. Make small filler blocks that shim out the box wall thickness. See **Photo No. 6**.

5. Use the rabbeting bit set-up that is closest to the width of rabbet cut required. For example, when using a bit that will cut a ¼" rabbet, temporarily shim out the wall thickness 3⁄32" all around with small shims held in place with double faced tape. The remaining outside lip will be 5⁄32".

6. Before rabbeting the lid, use a belt or disc sander machine to give the adjoining flats of the octagon box and lid a ⅝" connecting radius. See **Photo No. 7**. Again, make a test run with one of the prepared scrap pieces.

7. Assure that the lid fits, but not too tightly. Mount the fretted pattern to the lid with temporary bonding adhesive for scroll-sawing. Tip-place a ⅝" or ¾" thick filler block into the lid cavity while scrolling. The extra cutting thickness provides slower, but more controlled cutting.

8. Round-over the top and bottom edges with a ¼" radius bit, sand all surfaces, and finish.

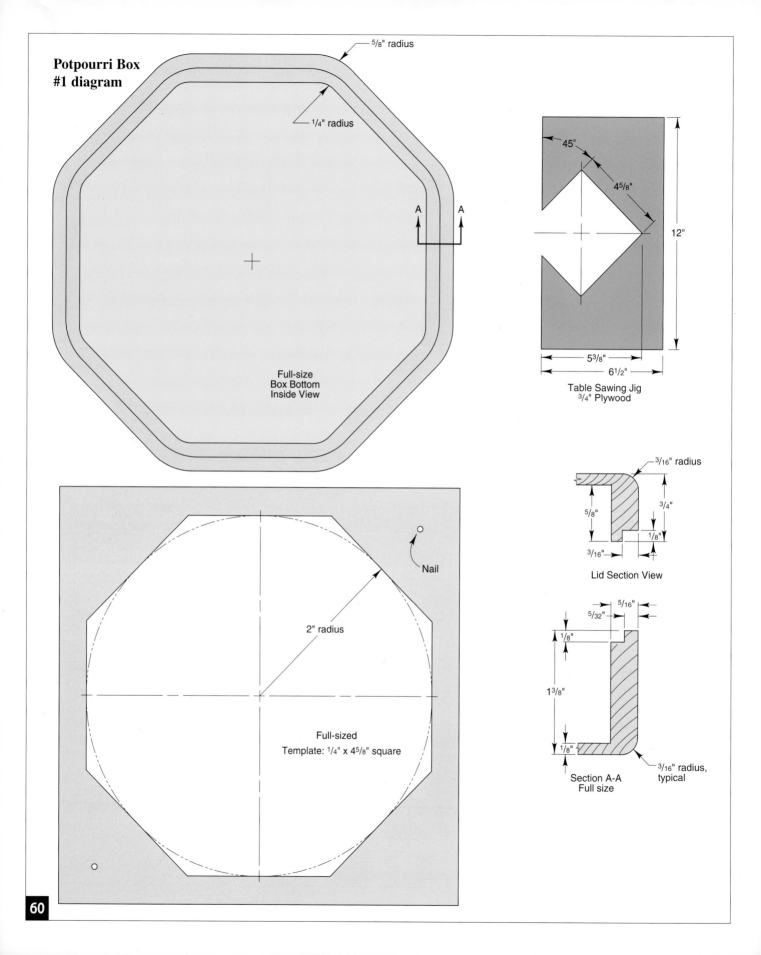

Potpourri Box
#1 diagram

⁵/₈" radius

¹/₄" radius

A A

Full-size
Box Bottom
Inside View

45°

4⁵/₈"

12"

5³/₈"

6¹/₂"

Table Sawing Jig
³/₄" Plywood

Nail

2" radius

Full-sized
Template: ¹/₄" x 4⁵/₈" square

³/₁₆" radius

³/₄"

⁵/₈"

¹/₈"

³/₁₆"

Lid Section View

⁵/₁₆"

⁵/₃₂"

¹/₈"

1³/₈"

¹/₈"

³/₁₆" radius,
typical

Section A-A
Full size

60

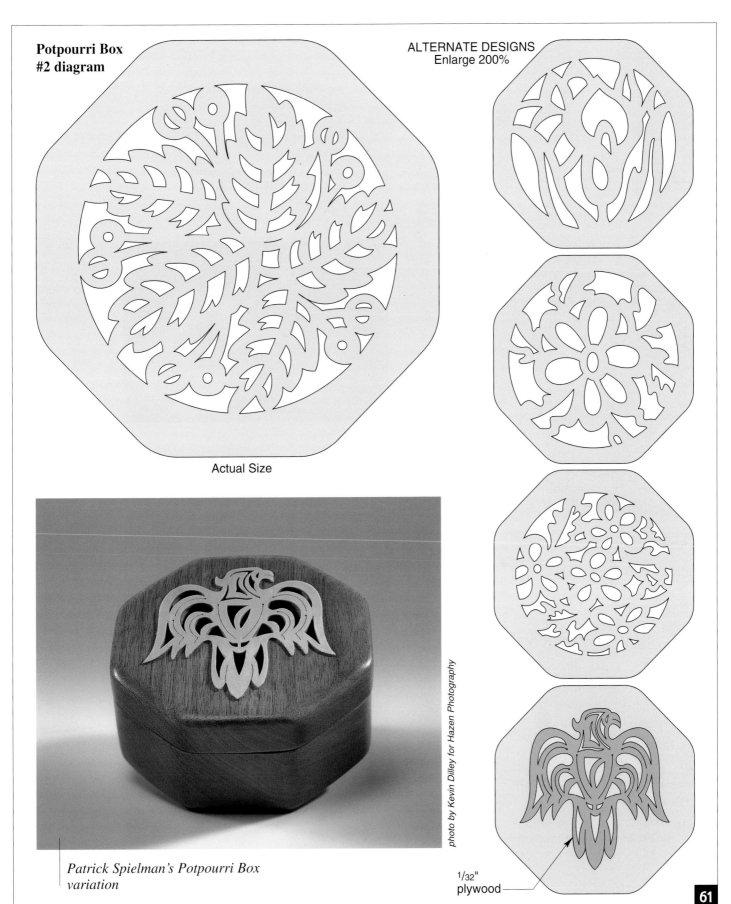

**Potpourri Box
#2 diagram**

Actual Size

ALTERNATE DESIGNS
Enlarge 200%

*Patrick Spielman's Potpourri Box
variation*

1/32"
plywood

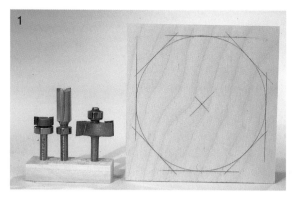

Photo No. 1. Some of the bits used for the Potpourri Box are from left to right: ⅝" diameter, x ¼" or ⅜" cutting length pattern bit, ½" diameter x 1" cutting length pattern bit, and a rabbeting bit. Note the ¼" plywood template layout ready for the scroll saw.

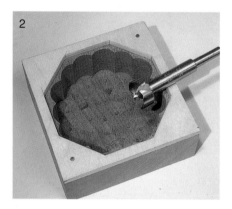

Photo No. 2. An optional step is to rough out the waste from the box and lid with a Forstner bit.

Photo No. 3. A pattern bit with a ¾" or 1" cutting edge is required for routing the inside of the box bottom.

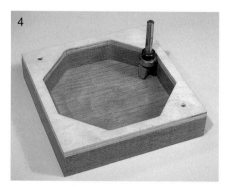

Photo No. 4. A pattern bit with a ¼" or ⅜" cutting edge length is used to rout out the lid, using the same template.

Photo No. 5. Jig used to cut the routed pieces from squares to octagons.

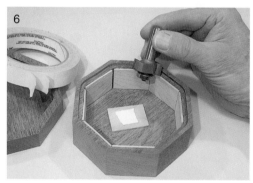

Photo No. 6. Shimming (with double face tape) to increase the box wall thickness permits rabbeting to a specific dimension depending upon the shim thickness.

Photo No. 7. Rabbeting the lid on the router table. Note the sanded radiused corners.

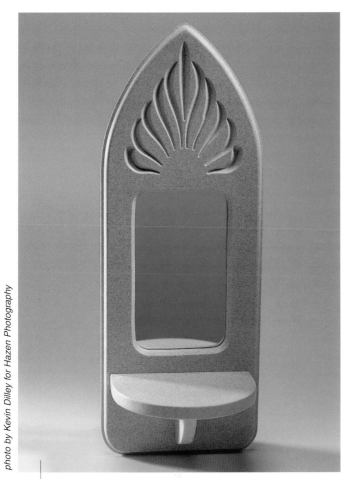

*Patrick Spielman's Carved Shelf,
Corian®,
½" x 6" x 16" H*

Carved Shelf & Clock

The surface router carving system described in
Chapter 5: Surface Routing beginning on page 29
is used to make the decorative incised designs on
these two projects. See **Photos No. 1 and 2**.

Carved Shelf Construction:
1. The shelf is made of ½" thick material, in this
instance Corian®. Solid hardwoods or other types
of solid surfacing material will also work nicely.
The first step is to carve the incised design using
"Jesada Tool's 3D Router Carver™ System." Just
one half of the "Blaze" furniture and drawer accent
template was used. Set ⅛" thick plastic mirror
material into a shallow rabbet with silicon adhesive.

2. Assemble the Corian® shelf and bracket pieces
using a gap-filling instant glue. Apply the glue to
one surface and moisten the mating surface with a
damp rag. See **Photos No. 3 and 4**.

Carved Clock Construction:
1. The carved clock is made of ¾"-thick hardwood.
Use a "Folklore" corner template to make the
incised carved detail around the clock insert.
Carefully position the template holding frame and
hold in place with double faced tape, on vertical
centerlines. Draw marks on the template holding
frame that bisect the corner design to help in
placing the template precisely for carving.

2. After positioning the template holding frame,
insert the template and mark the locations where
routing will occur using a pencil and a thin disc 1"
in diameter. See **Photo No. 4**.

*Patrick Spielman's Carved Clock,
mahogany,
¾" x 8½" x 12½"*

Photo No. 1. Mirror shelf of ½" thick Corian® with decorative incised routing.

Photo No. 3. Corian® shelf pieces ready for assembly. Note the bracket glued to the shelf, the instant glue, water and moist rag.

Photo No. 4. Spreading the glue on pencil marked lines onto which is placed the shelf assembly with water moistened gluing surfaces.

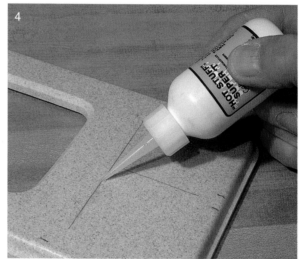

Photo No. 2. Routed clock plaque. The incised design was produced with a 90° corner design template, routed twice - once above the clock and once again below, with some overlap, which surrounds the clock insert with carving.

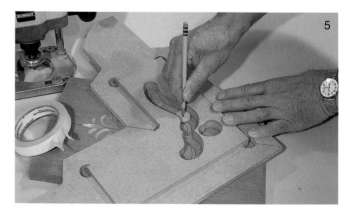

Photo No. 5. To preview and check the template position before actual routing, use a thin disc, 1" in diameter, with a small pencil hole following the template edges to mark the workpiece. Note the bisecting reference lines marked on the template holding frame.

Carved Shelf diagram

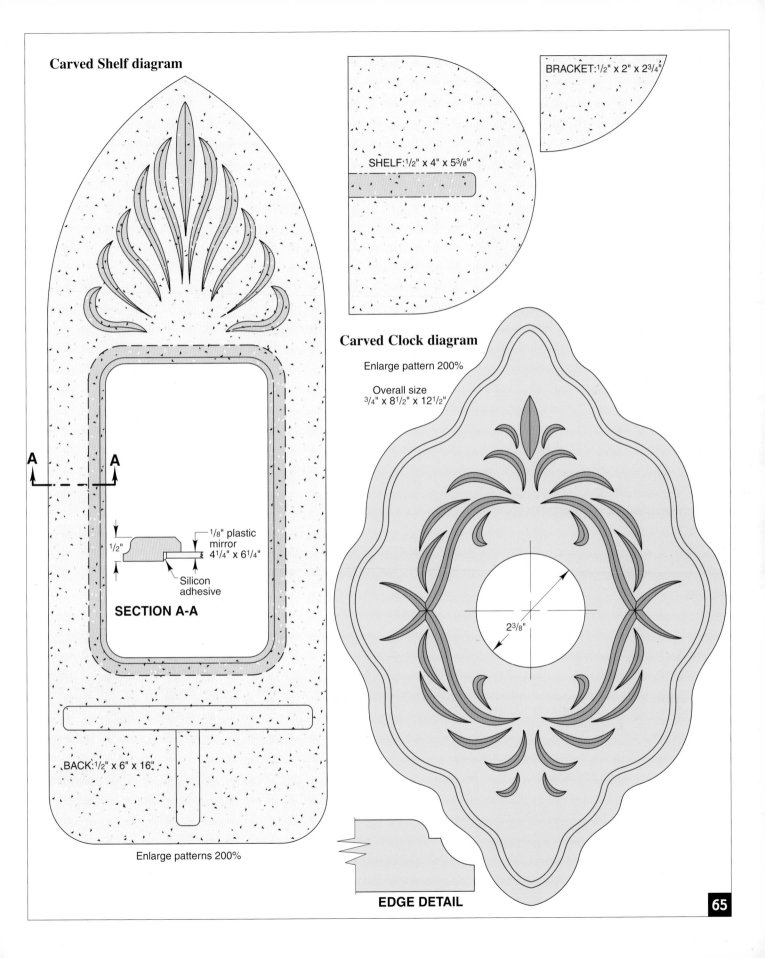

BRACKET: 1/2" x 2" x 2 3/4"

SHELF: 1/2" x 4" x 5 3/8"

Carved Clock diagram

Enlarge pattern 200%

Overall size
3/4" x 8 1/2" x 12 1/2"

A ◄—————► A

1/8" plastic
mirror
4 1/4" x 6 1/4"

1/2"

Silicon
adhesive

SECTION A-A

2 3/8"

BACK: 1/2" x 6" x 16"

Enlarge patterns 200%

EDGE DETAIL

Andy Anderson

Andy & Tracy Anderson

Andy and Tracy Anderson grew up on a farm in Spring City, Utah. They have loved working with wood as long as they can remember, and as kids, they would spend hours in their father's shop building "stuff." The only rule was that they couldn't turn on the big power tools—especially the table saw. So, when an adult wasn't around to operate the saw, Tracy would crawl under the saw and turn the blade by pulling on the belt as fast as he could while Andy cut the wood. Often times they had no idea what they were building when they started; they would simply design as they went along.

Andy and Tracy both took shop in junior high school and learned how to use those forbidden power tools, but that was about as far as their formal woodworking training ever went. In fact, Tracy was actually kicked out of high school shop for sword fighting—not exactly your model student.

The brothers' paths came together years later in California, where Andy owned and operated both an engineering firm and a large machine shop and Tracy was back in school getting a degree in electronics. Their love of woodworking

once again united, Andy and Tracy began to collect their woodworking tools and set up a shop just for fun. Little did they know their hobby was about to grow into something neither of them ever expected.

In 1990, Andy designed and built a milling machine for woodworking and called it the Woodchuck. In 1991, the brothers decided to try their hand in the ornamental mill manufacturing industry, so they moved back to Utah and started Phantom Engineering, Inc. Through experience and hard work, Andy has refined his milling system over the past six years. The latest design includes some very powerful features and is called the Legacy Ornamental Mill.

Although they are very busy building the business and developing new products, they still love to spend whatever extra time they have in the shop. Andy loves to build custom furniture. Most of his designs are his own. Even when he builds a traditional or period piece, he will change the design to fit his own style. Tracy, on the other hand, specializes in small projects, especially writing instruments.

Woodworking seems to be the common interest that has kept these brothers together. Perhaps they learned from a grandfather who showed them that few things in life are more enjoyable than creating something that people will cherish. At the age of 90, he built a blanket chest for each of his granddaughters and great-granddaughters, leaving a legacy that will last for years.

*Andy & Tracy Anderson's Hall Table,
Environ®,
48" x 15 D x 31" H*

Hall Table

The Andersons borrowed the traditonal design of a Queen Anne table, changed the style, and selected a new material to create this contemporary piece. They used one of the new solid surface materials called Environ®. This material, like most others, has no grain, so the thickness can be laminated in any direction. The entire project was made from one piece of Environ® 1" x 36" x 72" with some material to spare. Solid wood or other materials deemed appropriate could also be used.

Construction:

1. If building up leg stock, follow suggested sizes given on **Hall Table diagram** on page 68.

2. Make four identical legs using the Legacy ornamental milling machine.

3. Cut leg blanks to rough size with the band saw employing compound sawing techniques.

4. Cut legs to uniform size and shape using the ornamental milling machine and a template guided router.

5. Mill the outside curved corners in 10 passes at 9° intervals using an indexing head to achieve a shaped leg with 10 small flats around the 90° of the outside of the leg. Sand these small flats to form a round surface on the two outside surfaces of each leg.

6. Profile the flat insides of the leg using another template, but with the same basic router guiding technique.

7. Rout a decorative edge around the top and along the bottom edges of the rails.

8. Assemble the table.

Note: The legs could also be shaped in a variety of other ways. One method is to use a box jig (holding the leg) with a top mounted template to guide the router carrying a straight bit. The outside corners can be rounded over using a shop made convex shaped router base with a piloted bit. Some hard work, however, will be realized because the size of the round-over radius gradually reduces as it progresses from top to bottom. The dovetail tenons and open mortises can be cut on the router table.

Tracy Anderson

Andy & Tracy Anderson's Hall Table, Environ®, 48" x 15 D x 31" H

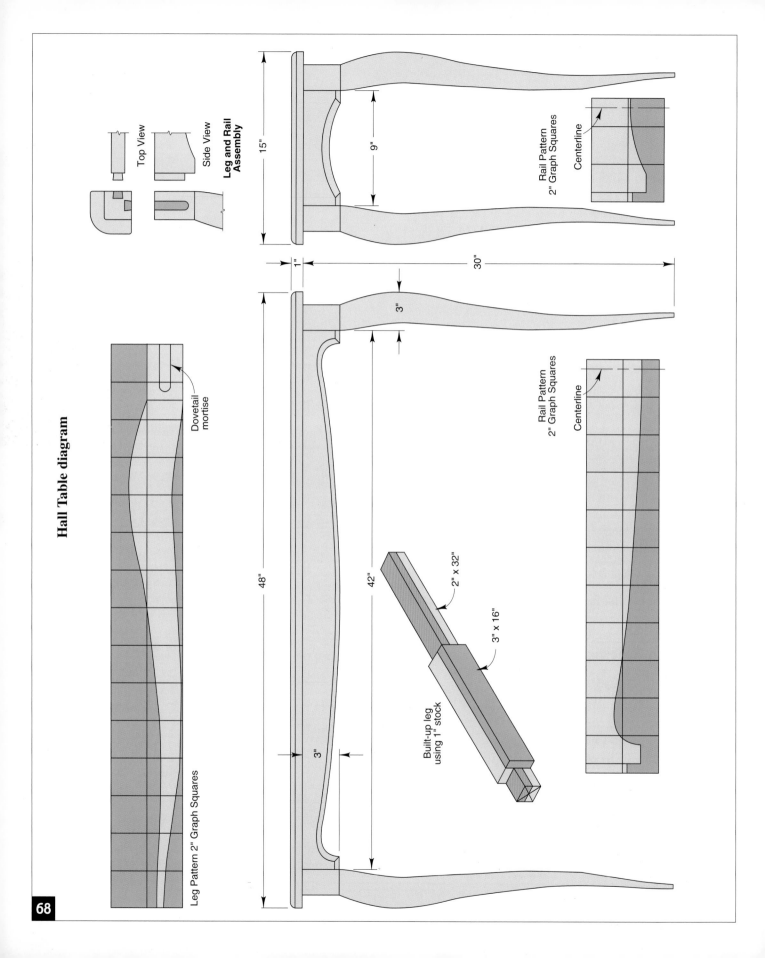

Hall Table diagram

Leg and Rail Assembly

Top View

Side View

Rail Pattern
2" Graph Squares

Centerline

Rail Pattern
2" Graph Squares

Centerline

Leg Pattern 2" Graph Squares

Dovetail mortise

Built-up leg
using 1" stock

2" x 32"

3" x 16"

15"

9"

30"

1"

3"

48"

42"

3"

3"

Andy & Tracy Anderson's Hall Table,
Environ®,
48" x 15" D x 31" H

Andy & Tracy Anderson's
The Cheyenne gallery piece,
antler

Andy & Tracy
Anderson's
The Executive
gallery piece,
maple burl

J. R. Beall

J. R. Beall has built and tinkered with things as long as he can remember. He has been a professional woodworker/ inventor since 1969. In the course of his nearly thirty-year career he has constucted harpsichords, kaleidoscopes, wooden machinery, bolt-together furniture, and faceted bowls. He has also designed woodworking equipment and holds two patents for his designs.

Much of J. R.'s work is done on specially adapted metal working machinery. Only two of his ten lathes were specifically designed for wood. Although he has been inspired by the Industrial Revolution and likes to think of his work as "low-tech," he often uses computer-controlled equipment to achieve precise results—designing it himself when necessary.

J. R.'s fascination with things that work has led him to explore wood threading methods and to develop a router accessory which produces precise threads on a variety of woods. The resulting wooden nuts and bolts have been included in many of his designs.

J. R. has a shop and tool business on his family farm in Newark, Ohio.

The Beall Adjustable Stool

Construction:

1. The seat is 1¼" stock shaped by using a router with round-over bit.

2. Glue the seat mount to the center of the seat extending the hole part way into the bottom of the seat for added support.

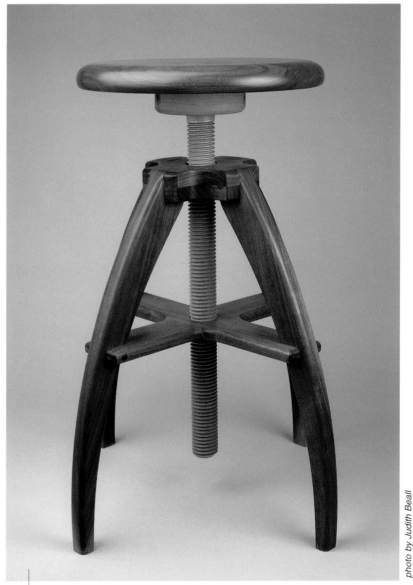

J. R. Beall's The Beall Adjustable Stool,
walnut with maple thread,
19" W at base x 20–30" H

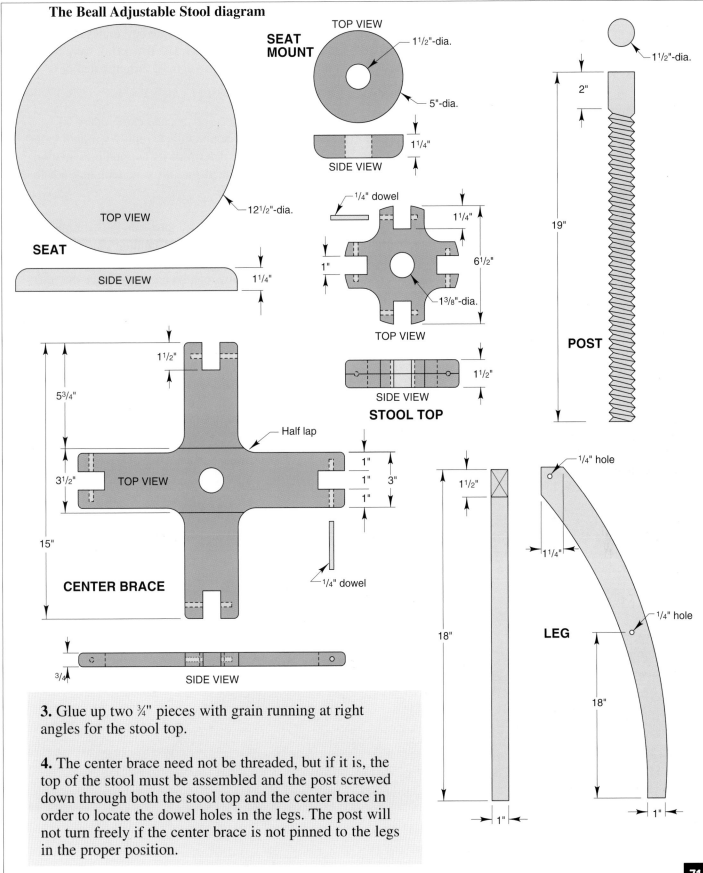

The Beall Adjustable Stool diagram

SEAT MOUNT

TOP VIEW

1¹⁄₂"-dia.

5"-dia.

SIDE VIEW

1¹⁄₄"

SEAT

TOP VIEW

12¹⁄₂"-dia.

SIDE VIEW

1¹⁄₄"

¹⁄₄" dowel

1¹⁄₄"

6¹⁄₂"

1"

1³⁄₈"-dia.

TOP VIEW

STOOL TOP

SIDE VIEW

1¹⁄₂"

1¹⁄₂"-dia.

2"

19"

POST

CENTER BRACE

TOP VIEW

1¹⁄₂"

5³⁄₄"

3¹⁄₂"

Half lap

1"
1"
1"

3"

¹⁄₄" dowel

15"

SIDE VIEW

³⁄₄"

1¹⁄₂"

18"

1"

LEG

¹⁄₄" hole

1¹⁄₄"

¹⁄₄" hole

18"

1"

3. Glue up two ¾" pieces with grain running at right angles for the stool top.

4. The center brace need not be threaded, but if it is, the top of the stool must be assembled and the post screwed down through both the stool top and the center brace in order to locate the dowel holes in the legs. The post will not turn freely if the center brace is not pinned to the legs in the proper position.

Peter Czuk

Peter Czuk began woodworking in northern California where he was moved by the texture and beauty of redwood burl. Now a resident of Michigan, Peter finds equal inspiration in the patterns of maple burl and spalted maple. His studio occupies the 1906 Kendall Town Hall were he is currently working on contemporary sculptural furniture and desk accessories.

Peter sees his clocks, letter openers, boxes, and cardholders, as exquisite expressions in wood. Each item is carefully wrought to let the unique character of the piece determine its use and presentation. The result is a lyrical line of products that resonate with individuality, each piece striking its own note.

Peter's creative challenge is to find new expression in traditional materials. "I like working on new designs of familiar objects. Take, for example, a traditional coffee table. It is basically four legs and a top. I think about how many shapes can be used to replace the four leg concept and still be a functional table. Then the challenge is connecting the shapes in a cohesive balanced form. A table can be seen from many different angles so there are a lot of view points to consider. I'm continually looking for what hasn't been done and have not hit a dead end yet. Success to me is finding a new twist on a familiar object and to have someone else recognize it too."

Peter Czuk's Free Form Routed Boxes, spalted sugar maple and maple burl, 5¼" L x 2¾" W x 1¾" H

Free Form Routed Boxes

Construction:

1. Select block of wood in desired size. Maple burl from Oregon and Spalted Sugar Maple from Michigan were used. Square the wood and cut off the lid, using a band saw.

2. A clamp jig fixture was designed using a workmate working bench. This enabled making a uniform lip all around various block sizes from 2" x 2" to about 6" x 10". The first cut defines the lip for the rabbeted lid, about ⅛" deep, using a Milwaukee router with a ½" double flute flat cutter.

3. The next step is to decide what type of interior partitions are desired, the only restraint being to keep it in a ½" radius at the inside corners. Once the rough form is established, rough out approximately 80% of the wood.

4. Use a high speed steel ½" cutter with a ¼" radius on the tip to work the final inside shape. This produces a soft radius where the sides meet. The high speed steel gives a sharper edge over the carbide tip. Periodically hand-hone the edge to minimize tear out.

5. The inside of the box is hand-sanded with Fordom flexible rotary sanding tools. Finish by hand with 320 grit paper.

6. The lid is rabbeted with a flat cutter against an adjustable fence on the router table. Micro-adjust the fence to fit the lid to the body. Finally, round-over the outside edges of the lid.

Peter Czuk's Free Form Routed Boxes, 6" L x 3" W x 1½" H

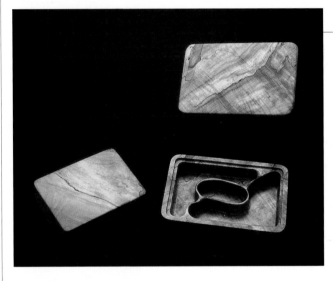

Peter Czuk's Free Form Routed Boxes, 5" L x 3" W x 1½" H

Peter Czuk's Free Form Routed Boxes, 5" L x 2½" W x 1½" H

photo by Diane Greenup, Vancouver, Canada

Jeff Greenup

Born and raised in the village of Caldbeck, in the English Lake District, Jeff Greenup is the fifth generation of his family to be involved in the woodworking and furniture trade.

His initial involvement with woodworking was through his father and grandfather, who operated the family business from a converted 18th century flour mill (originally owned by the local church) and utilized the existing water wheel to power their machinery. Jeff feels that this instilled in him an understanding and respect for time-honored construction methods and functional design.

Jeff operated his own custom furniture business in England between 1981 and 1989 which involved a wide variety of projects, including traditional pine furniture, chairmaking, antique restoration, and contemporary custom furniture. During this time, Jeff also spent two years attending Shrewsbury College of Arts and Technology and graduated with advanced City and Guilds of London qualifications in traditional furniture construction and design, including country chairmaking;

his work being exhibited and sold in galleries throughout England and Scotland.

Since the fall of 1989, Jeff and his wife Diane have lived and worked in Vancouver, Canada. He feels that his firsthand exposure to the North American craft furniture business has broadened his design thinking and appreciation of diverse furniture styles and construction techniques.

Jeff is currently working with Leigh Industries, the router jig company, helping them to develop jig applications and joinery. Leigh jigs were used on the four featured pieces as part of that program.

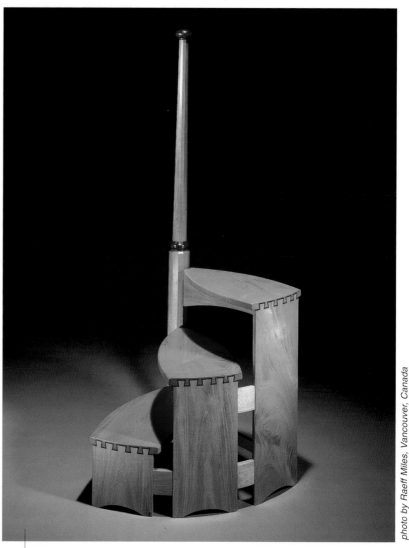

photo by Raeff Miles, Vancouver, Canada

Jeff Greenup's Library Step,
Honduras mahogany with cocobolo accents,
56" H x 20" radius of step x 8", 16", and 24" tread heights

Library Step, Chest on Stand, Desk Organizer, & Bookshelf

"A large part of my motivation to become a designer craftsman was to emulate the honesty of design and construction that is evident in quality craftwork from the past, without being restricted only to traditional furniture forms.

"While I have great admiration for past craftsmen and women who produced work of such beauty and longevity with only simple hand tools and often working in far from ideal conditions, I also realize that they were utilizing the most advanced tools and techniques of their day. They were not employing outdated tools and methods in order to be classed "traditionalists."

"Therefore, although my furniture background and training were very traditional, I do not have a problem using today's technology, ie: electronic routers and jigs, in my work—especially when combined with conventional jointing methods such as dovetails and box joints etc.

"In my work I strive to achieve a balance between function, design, and thoughtful use of quality materials, while maintaining my personal commitment to quality construction methods.

"It would seem common sense to me that building furniture to last for generations is a lot more resource efficient than pieces produced with an intended life span similar to, or even less than, that of today's automobiles."

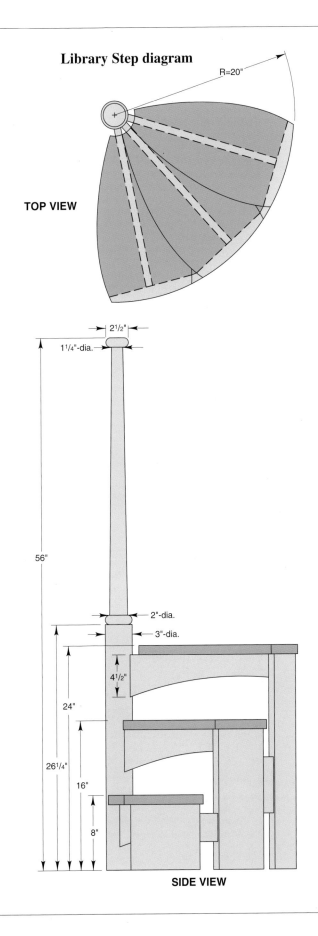

Library Step diagram

R=20"

TOP VIEW

2 1/2"

1 1/4"-dia.

56"

2"-dia.

3"-dia.

4 1/2"

24"

26 1/4"

16"

8"

SIDE VIEW

Jeff Greenup's Chest on Stand, Honduras mahogany, cherry, and African blackwood handles, 21½" W x 15½" D x 50" H

photo by Raeff Miles, Vancouver, Canada

Jeff Greenup's Desk Organizer, cherry and cocobolo, 23¾" W x 10⅞" D x 8⅞" H

Chest on Stand diagram

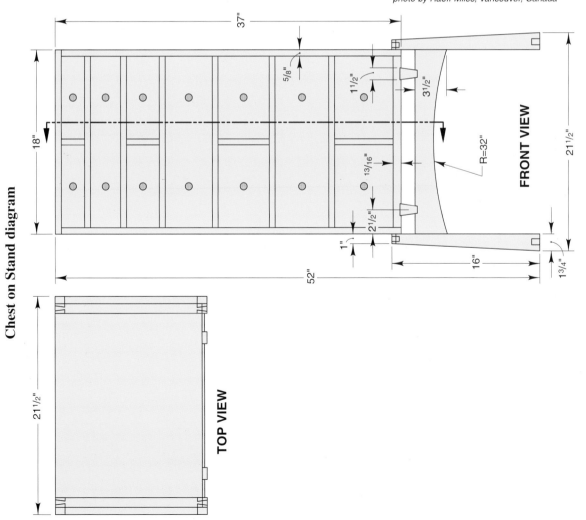

37"

5/8"

1½"

3½"

13/16"

2½"

1"

18"

R=32"

52"

21½"

1¾"

16"

FRONT VIEW

21½"

TOP VIEW

Chest on Stand diagram

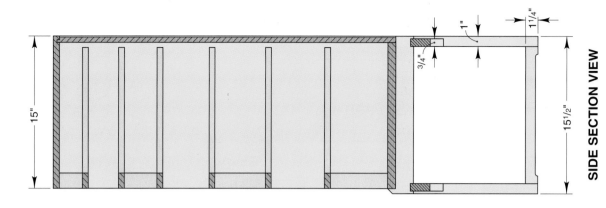

15"

3/4" 1" 1 1/4"

15 1/2"

SIDE SECTION VIEW

Desk Organizer diagram

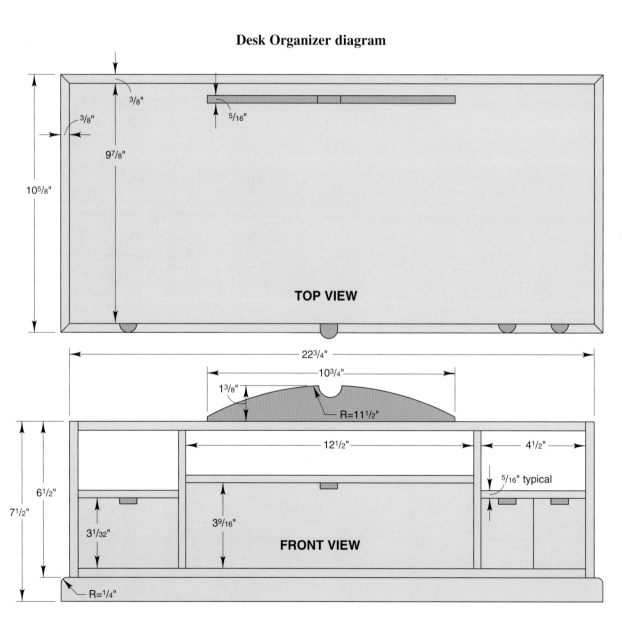

3/8"

3/8"

5/16"

9 7/8"

10 5/8"

TOP VIEW

22 3/4"

10 3/4"

1 3/8"

R=11 1/2"

12 1/2"

4 1/2"

5/16" typical

6 1/2"

7 1/2"

3 1/32"

3 9/16"

FRONT VIEW

R=1/4"

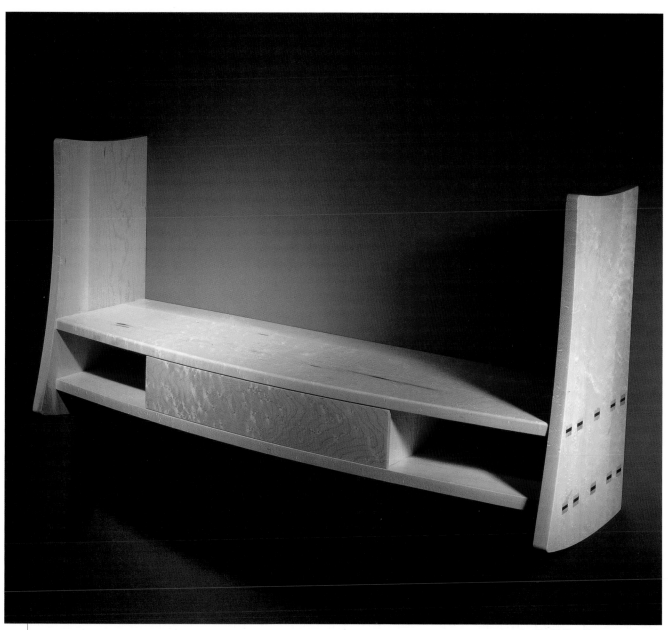

photo by Raeff Miles, Vancouver, Canada

Jeff Greenup's Bookshelf,
birdseye maple, maple, and cocobolo wedges,
32⅛" W x 9¼" D x 16" H

Bookshelf diagram

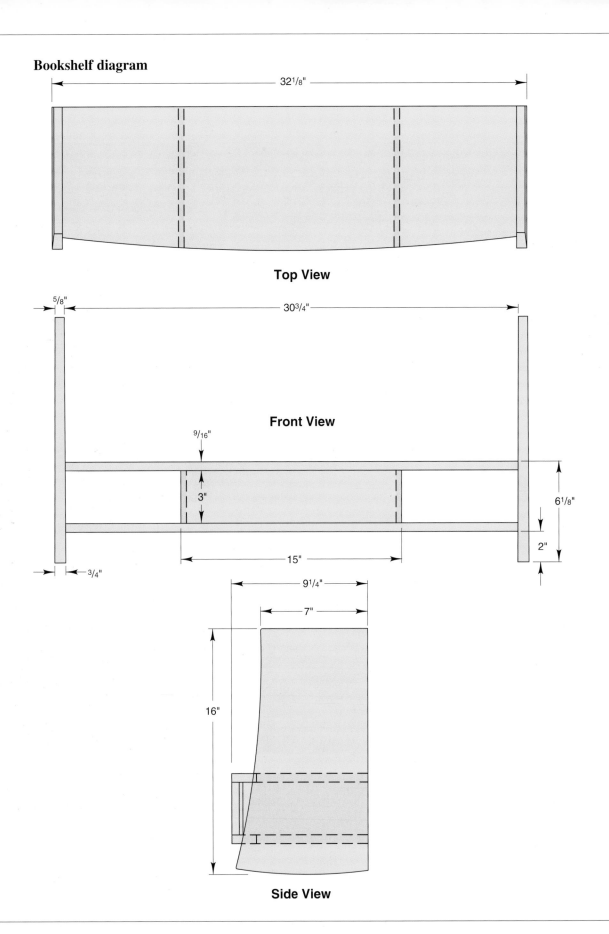

Top View

Front View

Side View

Michael & Rebecca Jesse

Jesse Woodworks has been in business since 1979. A husband and wife team, Michael and Rebecca design and build custom furniture in a studio located behind their home just outside of Salem, Oregon. Their business has evolved from cabinetry and built-ins to more and more furniture, which is now their specialty.

Michael has a degree in education and is a journeyman carpenter. He has taught in the construction program at Linn-Benton Community College. Michael is also a founding member of the Guild of Oregon Woodworkers and does occasional teaching. His design preferences tend toward contemporary with natural finishes and a passion for figured woods. Other interests include gardening, tropical fish, and officiating high school football.

Rebecca is originally from the midwest and met Michael while studying for her degree in interior design, with a concentration in furniture history. Two of Rebecca's favorite styles are American Federal and Queen Anne. Before joining Michael full time at Jesse Woodworks, Rebecca was a designer in an architectural firm, a cabinet shop, and a sawmill design firm. She also enjoys organic gardening (except for slug bait) and loves hiking and waterfalls.

The Jesse's have two children, a boy and a girl, and enjoy working at home where they can see and be involved in the whole life activities of making a living, learning, and enjoying life. "It is a good thing to be alive in America and have the opportunity to be creative and develop skills and be independent."

photo by Eric Griswold

Michael & Rebecca Jesse's Blanket Chests,
cherry, walnut, and maple with cedar trays and bottom,
approximately 18" H x 18" x 42"
Sculptural marquetry inlay on chest in foreground is by
Tom Allen at Joy of Doing, Silverton, Oregon.

Blanket Chests

The Jesse blanket chests feature Keller Jig routed dovetail exposed corner joinery, raised panel tops, rounded over corners, grooving, rabbeting, and other router work. The final duplicate profiling of the foot (base) pieces is accomplished using basic template routing techniques. The Jesse's prefer to use Native American hardwoods, especially Eastern cherry, Western walnut, and figured big leaf maple.

Construction:

1. Prepare long lengths of edge-glued stock so that the grain will continue to flow or wrap around the chest from the front to the ends (sides). Cut the four base pieces from one length of wood so the grain will follow in a continuous wrap around the chest. See **Blanket Chests diagram** below.

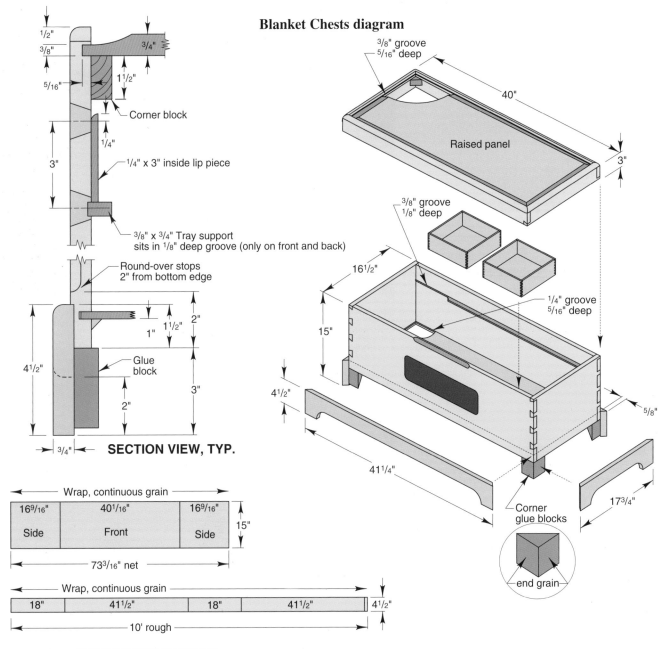

Blanket Chests diagram

1/2"
3/4"
3/8"
5/16"
1 1/2"
Corner block
1/4"
3" — 1/4" x 3" inside lip piece
3/8" x 3/4" Tray support sits in 1/8" deep groove (only on front and back)
Round-over stops 2" from bottom edge
2"
1 1/2"
1"
4 1/2"
Glue block
2"
3"
3/4"
SECTION VIEW, TYP.

3/8" groove 5/16" deep
40"
Raised panel
3"
3/8" groove 1/8" deep
16 1/2"
1/4" groove 5/16" deep
15"
4 1/2"
41 1/4"
5/8"
Corner glue blocks
17 3/4"
end grain

Wrap, continuous grain

| 16⁹/₁₆" | 40¹/₁₆" | 16⁹/₁₆" | |
| Side | Front | Side | 15" |

73³/₁₆" net

Wrap, continuous grain

| 18" | 41¹/₂" | 18" | 41¹/₂" | 4¹/₂" |

10' rough

STOCK PREPARATION

2. Use ¼" aromatic cedar plywood for the bottom. Create an inside lip by adding a ¼" x 3" band of hardwood around the inside on top of the tray support.

3. Machining and assembly is basic woodworking. The top floats in routed grooves that are stopped on the long sides (front and back). Glue-assemble the front, back, ends, top, and bottom as a single unit. Cut off the lid later on the table saw. Make the lid kerf on the centerline of the second dovetail from the top edge.

4. Rabbet the chest box ⅛" x 1½" all around the bottom so it will rest on top of the base. Miter the base pieces to fit. Band-clamp and screw them to the chest from the inside reinforcing at the corners with glue blocks.

5. Also featured, are two square solid aromatic cedar trays, rather than one large one. Square trays fit regardless of how they go in and are more easily handled. Use small wood stops on the inside lip to keep the trays away from the lid hardware.

Occasionally, the Jesse's will contract with Tom Allen of "Joy of Doing" for adding some dimensional sculptural marquetry (intarsia) to their pieces. Note the Silver Creek dogwood with a zebrawood background in the photo on page 81. Inlay the marquetry on the front into a routed recess.

Finish the piece with oil, followed by a tung oil and polyurethane varnish blend. Leave the aromatic cedar unfinished for optimal scent.

photo by Kevin Dilley for Hazen Photography

*Mark Kepler's Mirror,
mahogany,
20" x 30"*

Mark Kepler

Running his part-time wood working business from a small shop he built next to his home in Rockford, Michigan, Mark Kepler recalls his early years as a craftsman. "I envisioned a future working with my hands and projecting my creativity onto wood." What Mark did not anticipate was not having a steady income. "The stress over worrying about how many pieces you need to sell to pay the bills takes some of the enjoyment out of the woodworking process."

So Mark opted for a full-time job with Steelcase Inc., a major manufacturer of office furniture, and chose to keep his woodworking at an enjoyable level. Mark concentrates on making jewelry boxes, curio cabinets, small glass-top tables and sleek "free form" mirrors.

One of the challenges Mark has to face is the fact that he has had diabetes since he was 16 years old. He is currently on a waiting list for a donor kidney and is undergoing continuous dialysis treatments. This disease presents an even bigger challenge in his woodworking business in that it has drastically effected his eyesight. Because Mark can't see all of the tiny scratches, he has developed a keen sense of touch and prides himself on his finish work. Mark uses an industrial sandpaper that is sticky on one side. He sticks it on his hand and "sands his brains out." As Mark reflects on his life and his medical condition, he says, "I'm thankful to be alive and woodworking is a gift I have—I enjoy it."

Mirror diagram

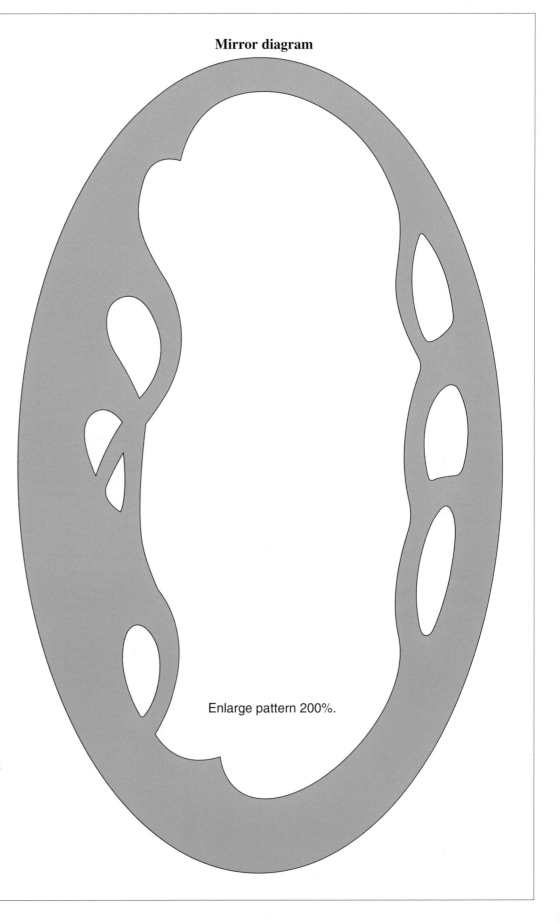

Enlarge pattern 200%.

Mirror

Construction:

1. Glue up stock ¾" thickness, three or more pieces to overall size of 21" x 34" or to suit, if modifying size.

2. Prepare ¼" thick tempered hardboard or plywood pattern.

3. Screw or nail template to back side of the wood.

4. With a ⅜" diameter straight or spiral bit and ¹³⁄₃₂" I.D. template guide attached to router base, cut the profile shape.

5. Remove template.

6. Round-over all edges ½" radius.

7. Sand entire frame.

8. Apply finish of choice.

9. Cut double strength ⅛" or ¼" plate mirror to suitable size and shape.

10. Attach mirror clips and sturdy wire hanger.

photo by Mary Sorenson

Russ Larson

Russ Larson developed his skills while earning a degree in Forestry Wood Products Management from the University of Missouri. He lives on his 780 acre farm in rural Nebraska with his wife, Irene, and two children, Jared and Trisha. Russ divides his time between raising his kids (as well as corn and soybeans) and designing wood creations for his business, The Wooden Gem. He also finds the time to teach Tae Kwon Do and run an outboard motor sales and repair business.

photo by Kevin Dilley for Hazen Photography

Russ Larson's Hourglass,
padauk,
6" DIA x 9½" H

His many designs include hourglasses of exotic hardwoods and hand-blown glass, one of a kind wooden musical instruments, elegant wood jewelry, and other custom items. Russ prefers to work with a variety of woods including zebrawood, cocobolo, ebony, Macassar ebony, birdseye maple, walnut, cherry, and oak. He handrubs his pieces with oil until the natural beauty of the wood shows through. Russ seldom uses stain, stating, "They (woods) are attractive just the way God made them."

Hourglass

Construction:
Note: Circle cutting jigs are very helpful in this project.

1. Cut two 6" diameter circles with the bandsaw out of ¾" wood of choice.

2. Rout the decorative edge around the circles.

3. Sand and finish the circles at this time. An oil finish is easiest to maintain.

4. Drill the three spindle holes 120° apart, ½" deep and ½"-diameter.

5. Drill center hole to fit hourglass. The hourglasses generally require a ⁹⁄₁₆" hole ½" deep.

6. Cut three pieces of spindle stock ⅞" square and at least 9" long.

7. Turn on a lathe, personalizing the design. For the model shown, an attachment was made for the lathe for routing the spiral in the spindles of the hourglass. Many other designs are possible with the router; fluting, etc. A Sears Router Crafter may be used, or other tooling. Be prepared to have longer spindle stock depending on what tooling is used.

8. Make sure the finished spindle is 8" long with ½" tenons that extend ⅜" beyond each end of the finished spindle. This will provide a total length of 8¾". Check the length of the hourglass to adjust the 8" one way or the other.

9. Finish the spindles.

10. Assemble the hourglass using felt or some other cushion material in the center hole. Use glue and assemble using a vise. It is advisable to do a dry run to make sure the glass fits properly. There should be ¹⁄₁₆" up and down play of the hourglass. Be prepared to modify the circles to accommodate the hand-blown hourglass.

The hourglass glasses are available from the artist or through various mail order catalogs.

Hourglass diagram

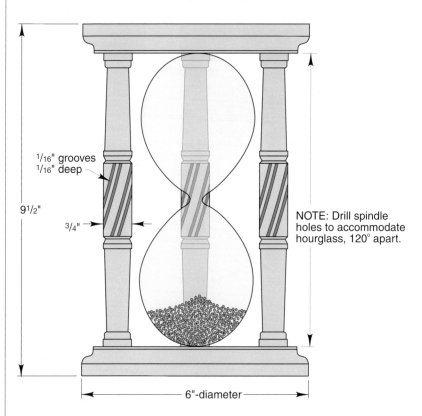

¹⁄₁₆" grooves ¹⁄₁₆" deep

9¹⁄₂"

³⁄₄"

NOTE: Drill spindle holes to accommodate hourglass, 120° apart.

6"-diameter

it with a small array of tools, he set forth to master his art.

Since then he has been featured in several publications, including the front page profile section of his local newspaper, various books and magazines, and has been nominated for numerous awards in his medium. He has attended some of the top retail and wholesale shows on the east coast, notably Lincoln Center in New York City and ACC Baltimore. His work is currently featured in more than 200 galleries across the United States, including Honolulu, Hawaii.

using simple hand tools; and continued through high school furnishing the homes of his family and friends. He then went on to college to receive his Bachelor of Science degree in Psychology—all the while making custom furniture to help pay his way through school.

While in college, Patrick received a near perfect score on the mechanical comprehension part of an IQ test. It was then that he realized that he might have a real knack for working with wood, instead of just using it as an avenue to earn money on the side. He set forth to earn his Ph.D., but loved working with wood so much, that he decided to forgo further schooling to pursue his craft. After designing and building his own studio (conveniently attaching a house to it), and equipping

Patrick Leonard's Moon Box,
birdseye maple and black walnut,
14" H x 13½" L x 7" W

Moon Box

The craterlike wood of birdseye maple and the sharp contrast of black walnut mimic the ominous feeling of the full moon piercing through the night sky.

Construction:
1. Begin with a piece of walnut ¾" x 6" x 50" and round-over the front edge ⅜" radius.

2. Cut a ¼" x ¼" rabbet into the back edge.

3. Miter-cut the board into four equal 12" lengths.

4. Cut a ¼" x 11" x 11" back.

5. Assemble the box using glue and band clamps.

6. Prepare the front material ⅝" x 10⁷⁄₁₆" x 10⁷⁄₁₆". Rout for a circle inlay ³⁄₁₆" deep x 6" diameter.

7. Prepare the moon inlay of birdseye maple. Glue and sand flush.

8. Rip the front into four equal pieces measuring 2⁹⁄₁₆" in width, using a fine kerf blade.

9. Prepare the drawers. Machine ½" wide grooves in the drawer sides. Dovetail corner joints.

10. Nail and glue ⅛" x ½" drawer guides to the inside of the box. Make and attach feet.

11. Sand and finish with Danish oil and lacquer.

Patrick Leonard's Oriental Chest of Drawers gallery piece, lacewood and black walnut, 14" H x 12½" L x 8" W

The design for the Oriental Chest of Drawers was inspired by the Japanese. The drawers with through dovetails slide on visible tracks, creating an openness which mimics Japanese architcture. Ring inserts and removable dividers make it ideal for any collection.

Moon Box diagram

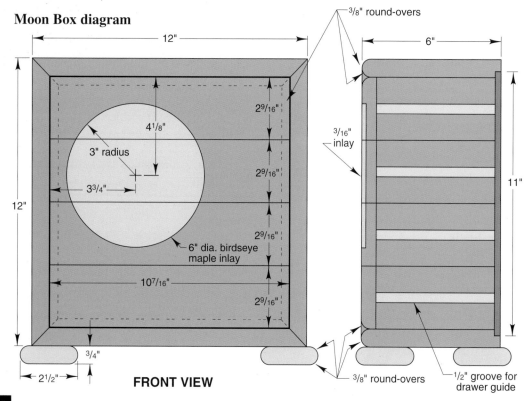

FRONT VIEW

SIDE SECTION VIEW

Perry McDaniel

Perry McDaniel's first experience with woodworking tools began in 1987 when he asked his father-in-law to help him construct a series of picture frames for some paintings he had completed. Though at the time the thought of actually pushing any wood past a cutter himself seemed completely out of the question, Perry eventually found himself scanning the newspaper and the local garage sale scene to acquire tools of his own. From picture frames, he moved to box making, and it was there that he discovered some of the real joys of woodworking.

With a full-time job as an illustrator, tool designer, and technical writer for Taylor Design Group Inc. (manufacturer's of the Incra line of woodworking tools), Perry's visualization skills have proved to be an asset in designing some of the many decorative joints featured in his boxes. "Shoptime for me comes at a premium these days. Raising three children with my wife in Midlothian Texas, while spending as many as 15 weekends a year traveling from coast to coast teaching others how to get the most out of their Incra equipment, keeps me pretty busy. In fact, I

generally produce no more than a handful of commissioned jewelry boxes a year."

The only pieces that Perry produces in any quantity are small puzzle boxes. Taking cues from puzzle box designs originating in the famous Hakone district in Japan, Perry combines boxmaking skills with devious, internal locking mechanisms to create some very intriguing small boxes. "I've been pleased with the reception that I've gotten from puzzle collectors around the world. It is a niche market with only a few specialty puzzle stores in Japan, Germany, and in the U.S., but it really helps to support my tool buying binges."

Perry has authored and illustrated two books: *The Incra Master Reference Guide* and the *Incra Jig Projects and Techniques* book featuring a few of his original box designs and box making techniques.

"For the future, I plan to continue experimenting with jewelry and puzzle box designs as well as teaching with more emphasis on one-on-one instruction, an area I've found immensely satisfying."

Photo by Marissa Wallace

Perry McDaniel's Stripes I, bubinga and hard maple, 9⅞" L x 6⅞" D x 3¾" H

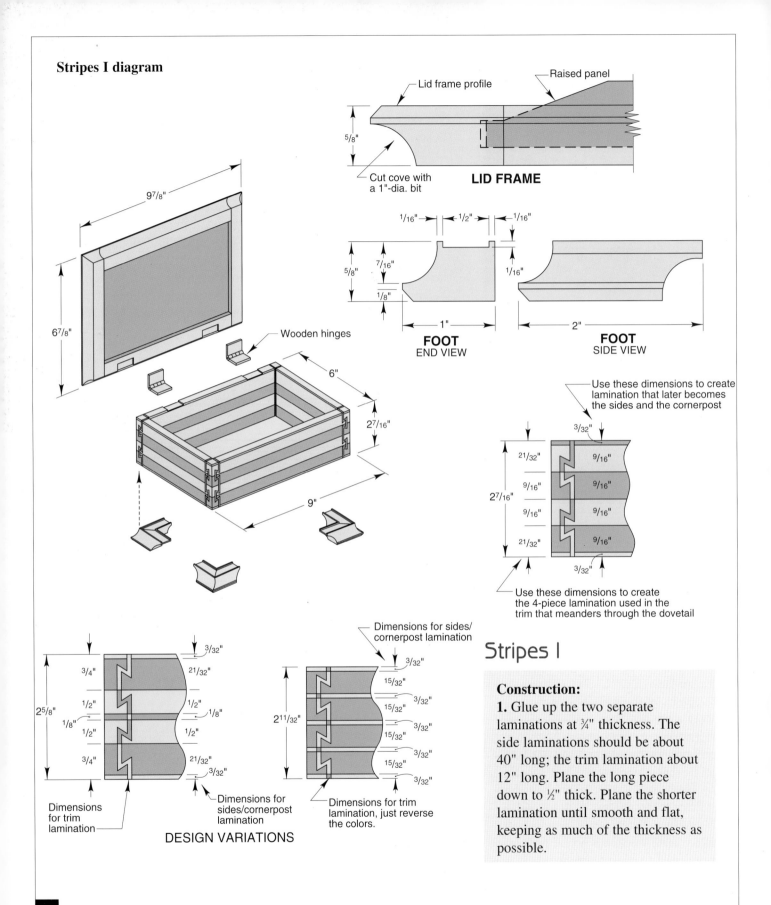

Lid frame profile

Raised panel

5/8"

Cut cove with
a 1"-dia. bit

LID FRAME

9⁷/₈"

6⁷/₈"

Wooden hinges

6"

2⁷/₁₆"

9"

1/16" — 1/2" — 1/16"

5/8"

7/16"

1/8"

1/16"

1"

FOOT
END VIEW

2"

FOOT
SIDE VIEW

Use these dimensions to create
lamination that later becomes
the sides and the cornerpost

3/32"

21/32"

9/16"

9/16"

9/16"

9/16"

9/16"

9/16"

2⁷/₁₆"

21/32"

3/32"

Use these dimensions to create
the 4-piece lamination used in the
trim that meanders through the dovetail

3/4"

21/32"

3/32"

1/2"

1/2"

1/8"

1/8"

1/2"

1/2"

3/4"

21/32"

2⁵/₈"

3/32"

Dimensions
for trim
lamination

Dimensions for
sides/cornerpost
lamination

DESIGN VARIATIONS

Dimensions for sides/
cornerpost lamination

3/32"

15/32"

3/32"

15/32"

3/32"

15/32"

3/32"

15/32"

3/32"

2¹¹/₃₂"

Dimensions for trim
lamination, just reverse
the colors.

Stripes I

Construction:

1. Glue up the two separate
laminations at ¾" thickness. The
side laminations should be about
40" long; the trim lamination about
12" long. Plane the long piece
down to ½" thick. Plane the shorter
lamination until smooth and flat,
keeping as much of the thickness as
possible.

2. Cut the four sides to length using the formula:

Side length (before joinery) = outside dimension - (2 x stock thickness) - $\frac{3}{16}$" + (2 x depth of cut)

Make certain to retain about 8" of the side lamination for use in making the corner-post pieces.

3. Set up the Incra Jig and cut the Incra corner-post double dovetail as described in the Incra Jig Projects and Techniques Book, using the IDDD template #38.

4. Cut $\frac{1}{4}$" x $\frac{1}{4}$" groove around box bottom to accept $\frac{1}{4}$" x $5\frac{3}{8}$" x $8\frac{3}{8}$" panel. Glue up box.

5. Using $\frac{5}{8}$" thick x $1\frac{1}{2}$" wide stock, cut the lid frame pieces to $9\frac{7}{8}$" and $6\frac{7}{8}$". Cut the $\frac{1}{4}$" x $\frac{1}{4}$" centered groove to accept a $\frac{3}{4}$" thick x $4\frac{1}{4}$" x $7\frac{1}{4}$" raised panel. Join the frame pieces using either a slip joint or a splined miter.

6. Using $\frac{5}{8}$" thick x 1" wide stock, cut the profile for the feet. The lid frame receives the same profile. Cut the $\frac{1}{2}$" wide x $\frac{1}{16}$" deep groove in the top edge of the foot then cove and miter-cut 2" long pieces of the foot stock for final assembly.

7. Hinge the lid to the box.

Perry McDaniel's Stripes I open, bubinga and hard maple, $9\frac{7}{8}$" L x $6\frac{7}{8}$" D x $3\frac{3}{4}$" H

Perry McDaniel's Stripes I detail, bubinga and hard maple, $9\frac{7}{8}$" L x $6\frac{7}{8}$" D x $3\frac{3}{4}$" H

Perry McDaniel's Night Stand gallery piece, hard maple, bloodwood and Gaboon ebony, 24" W x 17" D x 24" H

Perry McDaniel's Night Stand gallery piece detail, hard maple, bloodwood and Gaboon ebony, 24" W x 17" D x 24" H

Carol Reed

Carol Reed is a professional furniture builder from Ramona, California. Her shop in this rural San Diego county community is home base as she travels the United States assisting congregations in building their chancel furniture. She also conducts router workshops around the country. Recently, she has taught woodworking classes at Palomar Community College in San Marcos, CA.

Carol's woodworking interest was peaked by her grandfather when she was seven years old. One day, while trying to fix things around his farm, Carol's grandfather gave her a hand plane and taught her how to make pine "curly cues." While that task was undoubtedly designed to occupy his granddaughter and keep her out of his way, the spark of love for woodworking was struck that day.

Learning about woodworking was a frustrating experience restricted to learning from books and magazines until 1988 when she enrolled at Palomar College. The woodworking program there was and is one of the finest in the United States.

In addition to church furnishings, Carol designs and builds custom furniture. "I see myself more of a problem solver than woodworker when building custom furniture," says Carol. " Unique applications like computer work stations, entertainment centers, wall beds, specialized storage cabinets, and armoires are some of the things I like to do."

Most projects are made of domestic hardwoods, veneer plywoods, plastics and ceramics, decorated with hand carvings, turned finials, Gothic tracery, and feature hidden panels and concealed wiring for sound, lights, and video controls. The more complex, the better. Often the first question asked upon delivery of the piece is: "How many pieces are in this one?" Many times the answer is: "Hundreds."

Carol's work is marketed by the newsletter, The Churchmouse Gazette, and by speaking assignments in churches. Secular custom work comes by word of mouth.

She currently serves as Vice President of the San Diego Fine Woodworkers' Association. The SDFWA, at 1400+ members, is the largest woodworking club in the United States. She spends much time teaching on the college level, in local workshops, and at seminars around the country. She has contributed tips, tricks, and techniques to various woodworking magazines and is currently writing a book on utilizing vacuum technology in the woodshop.

Blessing Box

This box is designed to store a lock of hair, a graduation tassel, a first tooth, or any special little blessing of life.

Construction:
Make box joints as shown Blessing Box diagram on page 94. The shaded area shows where stock is removed to make the joint. Only two router bits are needed: ¼" spiral straight bit and ⅛" slot cutting bit.

1. Mill all stock to ¼" thickness.

2. Make corners ¼" box joints.

3. Make a ⅛" x ⅛" rabbet on both sides and one end of top.

4. Make a ⅛" x ⅛" rabbet on all four edges of bottom.

Note: One end is ¼" narrower to allow top to open.

Carol Reed's Blessing Box, cherry, 10¼" L x 5" W x 2¼" H

photo by Kevin Dilley for Hazen Photography

Blessing Box diagram

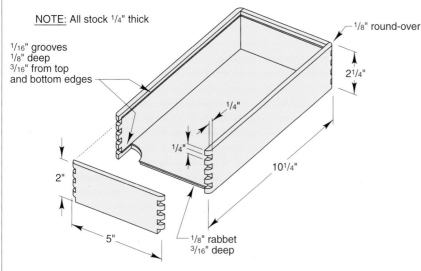

NOTE: All stock 1/4" thick

1/16" grooves
1/8" deep
3/16" from top
and bottom edges

1/8" round-over

2 1/4"

1/4"

1/4"

1/4"

2"

10 1/4"

5"

1/8" rabbet
3/16" deep

1/4" mushroom plug

1/8" rabbet
3/16" deep

10 1/8"

4 3/4"

Carol Reed's Baptismal Font, Honduras mahogany—stained Minwax mahogany red, 36" H x 28" W

This piece, owned by the Community Lutheran church in Escondido, California, has 208 pieces—all but eight were visited by the router. Even the hole the bowl fits in was routed with a trammel base.

The router was used on virtually every piece of wood, most interestingly, in forming the eight pieces that make up the top. Each side of each of the eight sections was fastened to a template. A straight pattern bit was used to remove material near the edges. That routed surface became the guide to remove the balance of the material using hand planes, scrapers, files, etc. while maintaining the overall desired shape of the top.

Carol Reed's Advent Wreath, Honduras mahogany—stained Minwax mahogany red, 7' H to top of Christ candle (the white center candle) x 42" across largest DIA

This piece, owned by the Community Lutheran church in Escondido, California, has 244 pieces—and all but 18 were routed. All the repetitive pieces were made using template routing techniques.

Bradford Rockwell

Although Bradford Rockwell is known to many as "the box man," he says making boxes was not in his plans when he attended an art school in Boston, Massachusetts. He studied illustration and cartooning and never took a single woodworking course. However, in looking back at some of his old cartoons, he notices an affinity for the box shape. Instead of drawing balloons around the words spoken by his characters, he used little expanding boxes.

After art school, he found himself living in a friend's woodshop, working for him one day a week in exchange for rent. Bradford learned how to make boxes to hold hand-rolled cigarettes. To appeal to a larger market, he redesigned the box to accommodate business cards or credit cards.

He worked for a time as a carpenter's helper and was then able to equip a shop of his own located in Saxtons River, Vermont, where, in addition to boxes, he has made wood briefcases, mirror stands, and cover plates for electrical outlets. One day, he says, for no particular reason, he made a set of four small nesting boxes. People loved them and wanted to buy them. So he pushed himself and made another set, even smaller, with six boxes. He went even further to produce his famous set of eight, which belongs to a collector in Walpole, New Hampshire.

Small Boxes

"Although my boxes appear to be little more than an example of simple tongue and groove joinery, they are actually the end product of a fairly complex process of hand-fitting each piece and matching wood grain.

"A hard wood with some kind of figure or design is carefully manipulated in the cutting process so that the grain matches from top to bottom.

"I cut most of the pieces too big and then sand them to a snug fit. I use a $\frac{1}{16}$" solid carbide double fluted router bit and some more unconventional "tools" in the construction process. A strip of masking tape helps to keep these very small pieces in place. A pencil serves as a push stick. Pipe cleaners are used to clean up glue in corners. Playing cards and dollar bills are used as thickness guides when fitting pieces together.

"Each box is put together in a dry run, clamped up for fit, and then taken apart again. Finally, it is put back together and glued up. The boxes are finished with tung oil.

"I do these as production pieces—but only about a half dozen at a time. Each has a lifetime guarantee."

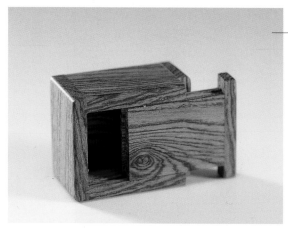

Bradford Rockwell's Ring Box, Mayan rosewood, 1¼" L x 1¼" W x ⅞" H

Small Boxes diagram

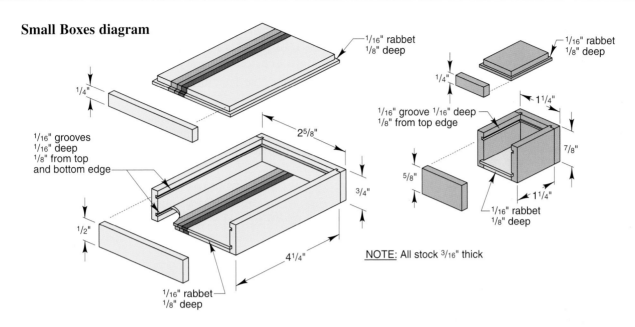

$^1/_{16}$" rabbet
$^1/_8$" deep

$^1/_4$"

$^1/_{16}$" grooves
$^1/_{16}$" deep
$^1/_8$" from top
and bottom edge

$2^5/_8$"

$^1/_2$"

$^1/_{16}$" rabbet
$^1/_8$" deep

$3/_4$"

$4^1/_4$"

$^1/_{16}$" rabbet
$^1/_8$" deep

$^1/_4$"

$^1/_{16}$" groove $^1/_{16}$" deep
$^1/_8$" from top edge

$1^1/_4$"

$7/_8$"

$5/_8$"

$1^1/_4$"

$^1/_{16}$" rabbet
$^1/_8$" deep

NOTE: All stock $^3/_{16}$" thick

Bradford Rockwell's Card Box,
walnut and cocobolo with padauk, ebony, tulip
wood, and cherry strips, 4¼" L x 2⅝" W x ¾" H

photo by Kevin Dilley for Hazen Photography

Gary Rogowski

In 1972, after what seemed like a lifetime of reading and studying for a degree in Literature, Gary Rogowski graduated with a B. A. behind his name and nowhere to go. But it was the '70s and the crafts revival was gaining steam. People were returning to crafts as a way of making a place for themselves in the world. Additionally, that place could be made starting out in your own basement.

Coupled with this movement in the industry was Gary's new-found fascination with objects. He had never taken woodshop in high school. His own knowledge of tools and materials was little to none. Yet, while at college, he met a group of physicists whose influence upon him was life-changing—if not life-threatening. He learned from them that everything was not extruded at a plant. He found out that the telephone poles and wires and the electrical impulses that traveled across the lines were products of imagination and sweat, not just another extrusion.

From them, Gary also learned about tools, motors, and carpentry. He took jobs as a Volkswagen mechanic, a tree trimmer, and a cement finisher. These experiences led him to the conclusion that working for a living was tough when you dream about creating things. So he quit his job, bought some tools, found some others, and began to build furniture.

At first, his work was rough but sturdy. The early standard was that if you could stand on it, it was strong enough. Gradually however, he taught himself the fine art of furniture making. In the process he has gained respect and success as he has built commissions for both public and private clients. His work has been shown at crafts fairs and art shows. He won an Oregon Arts Commission Fellowship. He built the library furniture for the Oregon State Archives. His carvings grace the Oregon State Forest Service. Galleries around the United States have displayed his furniture. Perhaps the most telling example of all is that for 23 years he has made a living as a maker of fine furniture.

Now his work is limited to special commissions, as the rest of his time is taken up with being a contributing editor for Fine Woodworking Magazine. His book and video, Router Joinery, have recently been published, and his classes and workshops for craft schools and woodworking groups around the United States are always in demand. His own school, the Northwest Woodworking Studio, began classes the summer of 1997 with a full schedule of workshops.

Walnut Stool

"I stole the idea for this stool design from a variety of sources. Tage Frid had a stool in Fine Woodworking Magazine in the early 1970s with a nice curve to the seat. I took that. James Knrenov was using gentle curves in the legs of his standing cabinets then. I liked those. The rest of the idea came from just playing with the angles of the legs and their footprint on the floor.

"Too often we forget to thank those designers and makers that came before us. We act as if we thought up our designs out of the ether—out of nothing—with no one to show us the way. Most everything that is done in woodworking, the Egyptians did 4,000 years ago. I am just happy I can steal their ideas and put them into my own shapes.

"This stool is the most challenging piece I build. And I have my router jigs finely tuned for cranking it out. Geometry is demanding of us—compound angles are even more so. This piece taught me patience, the value of careful planning, and how complicated it is to do something that looks so simple."

Gary Rogowski's Walnut Stool, walnut, 16" x 16" x 25" H

photo by Harold Wood

Walnut Stool diagram

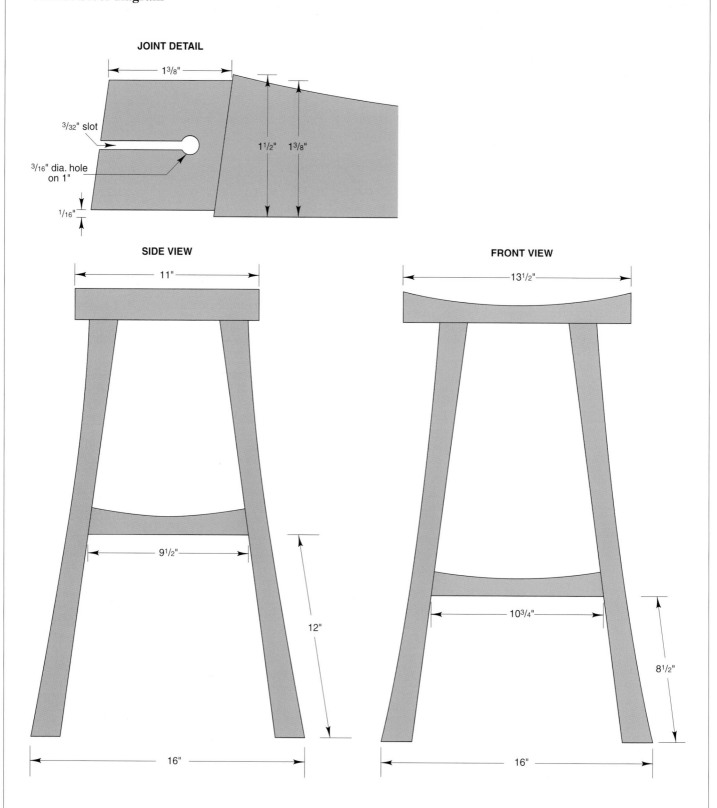

JOINT DETAIL

1³/₈"

³/₃₂" slot

³/₁₆" dia. hole on 1"

1¹/₂"   1³/₈"

¹/₁₆"

SIDE VIEW

11"

9¹/₂"

12"

16"

FRONT VIEW

13¹/₂"

10³/₄"

8¹/₂"

16"

John Schwartzkopf

John Schwartzkopf was born and raised on a farm west of Stuart, Iowa but moved into "town" during his 7th grade year of school. His father built houses and his mother managed a furniture decorating shop.

With his father's help, John started a woodworking hobby that would stay with him through life, building everything from model planes, rockets, and cars to whatever he could dream up in the shop.

John attended Iowa State University in Ames, Iowa spending two years in mechanical engineering, almost switching to architecture, and graduating with degrees in Philosophy and Anthropology in 1973.

His post college years found him doing more serious woodworking and doing commissioned work part-time. In 1980, he moved to Cedar Rapids and worked for an architectural millwork shop. When the shop closed, John found himself working full time in his own furniture business.

John works out of a large, one-man shop located behind his home where he does all of his own designing and construction. He still does mainly commissioned work, but has been doing an increasing amount of gallery work for several galleries located in the Midwest.

"I have spent my whole life building and designing things for my own enjoyment as a hobby. I feel fortunate that I can make a living at it as well."

Mirror & Shelf

This project combines wood (birdseye maple) with a new material called Environ® manufactured by Phenix Bio-composites. Other material combinations or all wood construction of choice can also be used.

Construction:
1. Check **Mirror & Shelf diagram** for specifications for the large radii of many of the curved pieces. Saw them to a rough size and then router-cut to final shape/size. See **Photo No. 1**. Use a shop-made trammel for easier cutting of the larger arcs and curves. There are some joints that have mating inside and outside radii, so work must be accurate. Rough-cut the end of the vertical components with a jig saw or bandsaw and sand to finished shape. See **Photo No. 2**.

2. Use a trim router to round-over all forward edges to a ⅛" radius. Use sandpaper to soften other sharp corners and the back edges. Sand all pieces before assembly. See **Photo No. 3**.

3. Connect the pieces using #20 biscuits. Assemble the two horizontal members at the outside ends of the mirror before cutting the ends to match the mating curves of the vertical pieces. The biscuit joiner will work on the curved joints because the curves are so slight. See **Photo No. 4**. Glue up the assemblies working from the center toward the outside, adding one section at a time. Tightbond II™ was used in the biscuit slots on the wood side and Environ® glue (or Gorilla glue) on the Environ® side. Do not use regular glue with Environ® as the joint will eventually weaken.

4. Notice the mirror section detail showing five small pieces screwed to the back which holds the mirror and plywood backer into the rabbeted lip.

5. Gradually off-set or lower the shelf components ⅛" from each other, progressively, from the largest center piece toward the ends. Cut shims of ⅛" and ¼" plywood to provide support underneath as appropriate. See **Photo No. 5**. Paint all exposed edges black. Mount the shelf to the wall using any suitable metal brackets available.

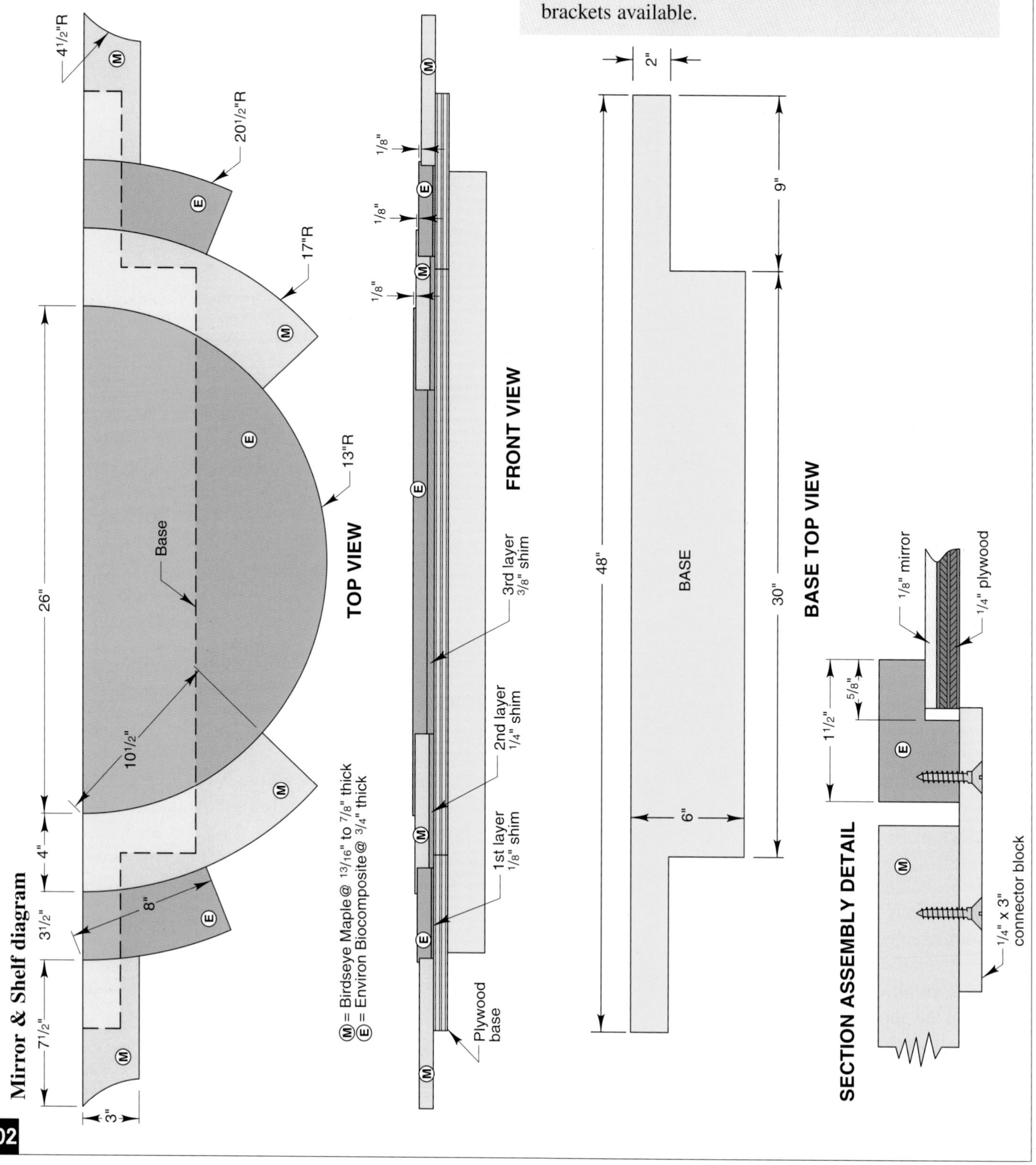

Mirror & Shelf diagram
TOP VIEW
FRONT VIEW
BASE TOP VIEW
SECTION ASSEMBLY DETAIL
M = Birdseye Maple @ 13/16" to 7/8" thick
E = Environ Biocomposite @ 3/4" thick
4 1/2"R
20 1/2"R
17"R
13"R
Base
26"
10 1/2"
4"
3 1/2"
8"
7 1/2"
3"
1/8"
3rd layer 3/8" shim
2nd layer 1/4" shim
1st layer 1/8" shim
Plywood base
2"
9"
48"
BASE
30"
6"
1/8" mirror
1/4" plywood
5/8"
1 1/2"
1/4" x 3" connector block

Photo No. 1. Plunge router set-up on a shop made trammel system to cut the very large radii curves. *Photo Courtesy: Strong Productions.*

Photo No. 2. Cutting part ends to a rough size. *Photo Courtesy: Strong Productions.*

Photo No. 3. Finish sanding before assembly. *Photo Courtesy: Strong Productions.*

Photo No. 4. Biscuits are used to join the pieces. *Photo Courtesy: Strong Productions.*

Photo No. 5. Inspecting the assembly and finish. *Photo Courtesy: Strong Productions.*

Mirror & Shelf diagram (cont.)

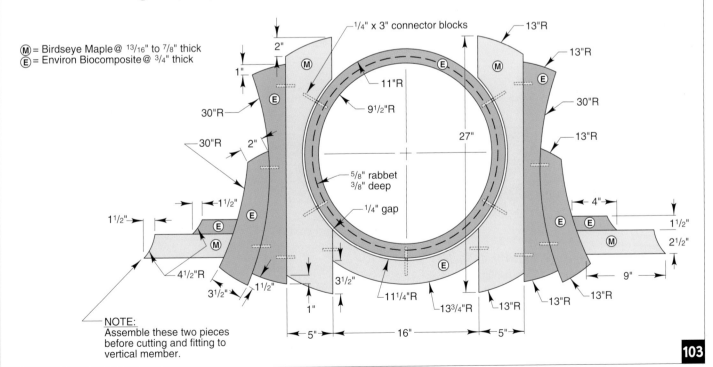

Ⓜ = Birdseye Maple @ $^{13}/_{16}$" to $^7/_8$" thick
Ⓔ = Environ Biocomposite @ $^3/_4$" thick

$^1/_4$" x 3" connector blocks

NOTE:
Assemble these two pieces before cutting and fitting to vertical member.

John Schwartzkopf's Mirror & Shelf,
birdseye maple and Environ®,
mirror: 56" W x 27" H, shelf: 13" D x 56" W

Japanese Serving Tables

"Designed specifically for a Japanese styled home, these tables feature an open frame/leg style that has become somewhat of a trademark of mine."

The essential structural details can be employed to make tables of any size desired. Simply change the dimensions as necessary. The leg detail involves basic mortise and tenon frame construction.

Construction:

1. Machine and assemble two end frames and two side frames for each table.

2. Make the leg spacer blocks and the top cove blocks in one continuous length of stock that can be cut into lengths later. Test-fit the cove block material to the top panel thickness. The fit should be snug, but still free enough to allow shifting or movement of the solid top material with changes in atmospheric moisture. If building in the winter, allow ⅛" on each side; in the summer allow less.

3. Glue the leg spacer blocks to the end frames before final assembly. Also, make a dry run assembly of the end frames to the side frames to check everything for the proper fit. Check to assure that space has been allowed for wood movement.

4. The final assembly is best made with the table upside down on a flat work surface. Prepare some plywood shims and spacers to help position everything at the correct elevations. Assure that the tip is centered in the assembled frame. Put just one screw through the center of each support, allowing the top to move but remain centered.

5. Finish by hand-rubbing several coats of Waterlox®, a tung oil based finish.

photo by Mike Mitchell

John Schwartzkopf's Japanese Serving Tables, solid cordia wood with wenge frame and legs, 11½" H x 11⅛" W x 32" L

Japanese Serving Tables diagram

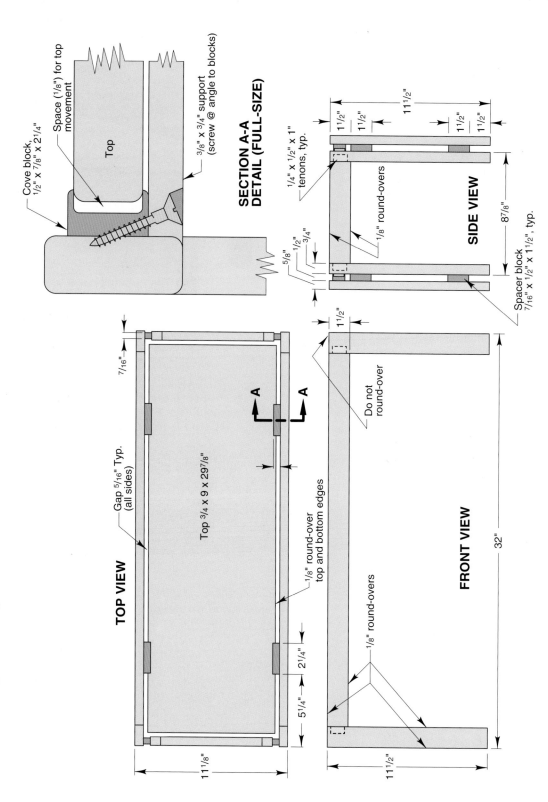

Cove block,
$1/2" \times 7/8" \times 2^1/4"$

Space ($1/8"$) for top movement

Top

$3/8" \times 3/4"$ support
(screw @ angle to blocks)

**SECTION A-A
DETAIL (FULL-SIZE)**

$1/4" \times 1/2" \times 1"$ tenons, typ.

$1/8"$ round-overs

$5/8"$ $1/2"$ $3/4"$

SIDE VIEW

$11^1/2"$

$1^1/2"$ $1^1/2"$ $1^1/2"$ $1^1/2"$

$8^7/8"$

Spacer block
$7/16" \times 1/2" \times 1^1/2"$, typ.

$7/16"$

Gap $5/16"$ Typ.
(all sides)

Top $3/4 \times 9 \times 29^7/8"$

TOP VIEW

A

A

$1/8"$ round-over
top and bottom edges

$2^1/4"$

$5^1/4"$

$11^1/8"$

$1^1/2"$

Do not
round-over

FRONT VIEW

$1/8"$ round-overs

$32"$

$1/8"$ round-overs

$11^1/2"$

John Schwartzkopf's Stately Reception Desk gallery piece close-up of details which involve much router work. The Avonite™ is inset or inlaid into the surface employing male and female template routing techniques.

John Schwartzkopf's Stately Reception Desk gallery piece, Honduras mahogany with birdseye maple, polished glass, and Avonite™ writing surface, 36" D x 39" H x 78" W

The glass is actually three shelves that come through from the back and appear here as three curved tubes between the gold leafed sphere turnings.

John Schwartzkopf's Java Table gallery piece, hardwood legs and bracing with Environ® top, 19" H x 25" W x 48" L

Features basic, but elegant lines with straight forward construction.

photo by De Sheldon

Daru Stevens

Daru Stevens taught high school English for 25 years, setting up his woodshop shortly after retirement. After a year of experimenting, he began making pieces designed around the fine-art capabilities of the Incra Jig, a tool-positioning device that makes repeatable accuracy possible. Since 1994, his work has been displayed and sold at the Jessel Gallery in Napa, California. Daru now builds only his own original computer-assisted designs. Three of his woodworking articles are being published in 1997.

Most of Daru's work is very practical jewelry boxes, emphasizing decorative joinery and utilizing exotic woods, and many of his pieces feature California bay from his own back yard and a variety of hardwoods salvaged from his neighbors' yards. His work is distinguished by his careful attention to detail. The featured Butter Dish was designed as a gift for one of his daughters while the jewelry box is one in his Pleiades series of boxes that reflect the world wide excitement about UFO's.

Daru credits his early success to the Incra Jig. "The really wonderful thing about these new positioning tools," he says, "is that they make it possible to create beautiful, intricate pieces with joinery that was not possible using traditional methods.

"Working with wood to high tolerances is demanding. I learn my limitations, I learn my machines' limitations, and I learn how to push them to achieve the maximum. And sometimes my limitations expand. That is very satisfying."

The Step Chest was inspired by Japanese tansu, but the use of exotic wood and decorative joinery departs from that tradition. The drawers lock when closed; the key to opening them is a magnet in the base of the sculpture.

Butter Dish

Construction:
1. Build-up a block for the cover (decorative). Use the Incra or Join Tech positioning devices, if available, as desired.

2. Trim the cover block to finished size.

3. Make routing template jigs for the dish and the cover.

4. Rout out the recess in the dish with a ¾"-diameter bit and the cover with a ½"-diameter bit.

5. Shape the cover exterior with a ⅜"-radius round-over bit. Bevel the dish bottom at the table saw, round the corners with sandpaper, and round the top edge with a ⅛"-round-over bit.

6. Sand and finish with Behlen's Salad Bowl finish. Let cure long enough to be food safe.

Pleiades Box

Note: Have the mirror cut to size first. If necessary, adjust the size of the top mirror template so the recess is slightly larger to allow for wood movement.

Construction:
1. Referring to **Pleiades Box diagram**, make the three large templates for: the bottom (#1), the top (#2 and #3), and the leg dovetail (#4) routing. (Note: the diagram for the templates #2

Daru Stevens's Butter Dishes, Left Cover: maple and angico—a heavy, hard South American wood, Left Dish: maple

Right Cover: zebrawood, maple trim, and purple heart center, Right Dish: zebrawood, 3½" W x 7" L x 3⅜" H

photos by Kevin Dilley for Hazen Photography

Daru Stevens's Pleiades, Left: rosewood and ebony

Right: zebrawood and ebony, 8" x 8" x 5" H

A specially designed wooden hinge features a stopper to keep the lid from falling back. Daru does the pattern for the bottom interior on the computer, glues it to the material to make a template, cuts the template very carefully by hand, and routes it out. The boxes sit on four legs that are dovetailed into the bottom, one leg in front and three in back.

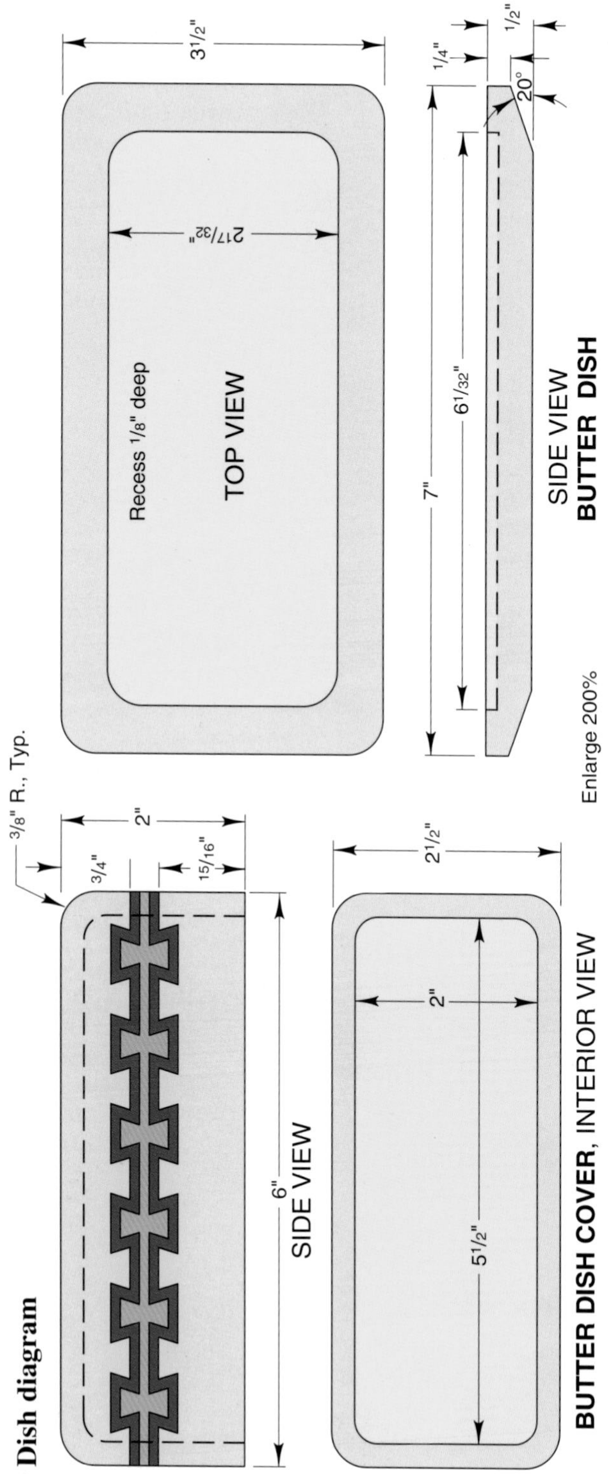

3½"
2 17/32"
Recess 1/8" deep
TOP VIEW
1/4"
1/2"
20°
6 1/32"
7"
SIDE VIEW
BUTTER DISH
Enlarge 200%
3/8" R., Typ.
2"
3/4"
15/16"
6"
SIDE VIEW
2½"
2"
5½"
BUTTER DISH COVER, INTERIOR VIEW

Butter Dish diagram

Pleiades Box (cont.)

and #3 are not given—#2 is a 7" dia. circle to be used with a bowl cutter and #3 is a 6½" circle to be used with a straight bit for the mirror).

2. Use bowl or dishing cutters with shank-mounted bearings to rout out the interiors of the top and bottom.

3. Rout the dovetail slots into the bottom for the legs. Cut the sliding tails in some leg stock to fit the cuts in the bottom. Rough-saw and shape the legs as desired. Note the legs should extend to the outside edge of the octagon. Finish-sand with the legs in place to assure a flush fit.

4. Rout the rabbets for the hinges and handle piece.

5. Make the handle. Cut it slightly oversize and note the grain direction.

6. Make the hinge following the Incra Jig hinge directions.

7. Assemble. Match the top hinge to the bottom hinge when gluing.

8. Shape the hinge to fit the octagon.

9. Sand the lift handle to a pleasant curve.

10. Finish.

Part / Materia1	**Quan.**	**T**	**W**	**L**
Top / rosewood	1	2"	8"	8"
Bottom / rosewood	1	2"	8"	8"
Hinge blank / rosewood	1	⅜"	6"	3"
Leg blanks / rosewood	4	¾"	1⅞"	1¼"
Handle blank / ebony	1	3⁄16"	4½"	1⅛"
Mirror	1	⅛"	6½" dia.	
Hinge pin / brass rod	1	⅛" dia.		3¾"
Templates:				
#1, #2, #3 MDF	3	½"–¾"	12"	12"
#4 MDF	1	¼"	12"	12"
Vertical frames / scrap	8	1½"	2"	12"
Horizontal frames / scrap	8	1½"	2"	8"

Pleiades Box diagram

CROSS SECTION
MIRROR, LIFT, and STOPPER HINGE

Mirror 6 1/2" diameter

3/16"

45°

1"

3/16"

Enlarge pattern 200% for full size

1 3/8"   1 1/2"

3/16"

7" diameter

1/4" round-over

LEG

1 7/8"   5/8"

1 1/4"   45°   3/4"

1/4"

1/2"   1/4"

Enlarge pattern 200% for full size

1 1/8"

2"

CROSS SECTION
FRONT and BACK LEGS and HINGE

7/8"

HINGE BLANK LAYOUT

END VIEW

3/8"   3/4"   1 1/2"   3/16"

3/8"

3/8"

Stopper   3/4"

1/4" x 5/8" x 7/8"
dovetail pins

Bottom
Leaf

4 3/4"

2 1/8"   2 1/8"

7/8"

Top
Leaf
1

3/8"
3/8"
3/8"

1 1/2"

1/2"

3/8"

Top
Leaf
2

3/8"
3/8"

3/8"

8"

3/8"
3/8"
1/2"

7/16"   7/8"

1/8" hole

3/8"
bull-
nose

3/8"

1 1/8"   1 1/8"

END VIEW

8"

Enlarge pattern 200%

BOTTOM LEG PLACEMENT

Enlarge pattern 200%

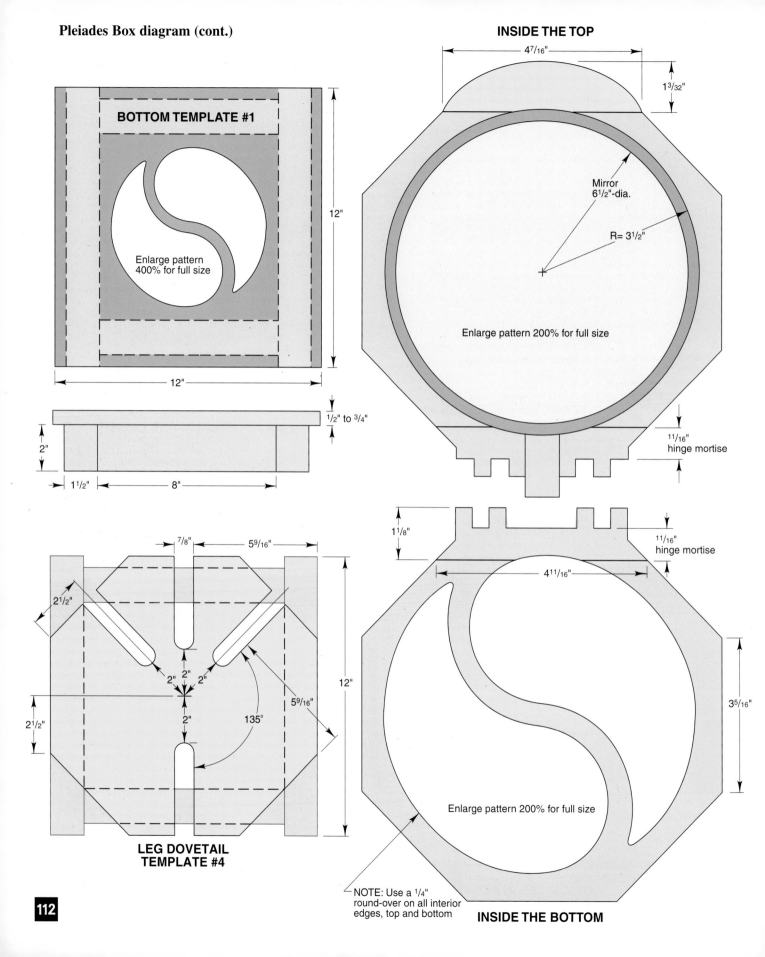

BOTTOM TEMPLATE #1

Enlarge pattern 400% for full size

12"

12"

1/2" to 3/4"

2"

1 1/2"   8"

INSIDE THE TOP

4 7/16"

1 3/32"

Mirror
6 1/2"-dia.

R= 3 1/2"

Enlarge pattern 200% for full size

11/16"
hinge mortise

7/8"   5 9/16"

2 1/2"

2" 2" 2"

2 1/2"   2"

135°

5 9/16"

12"

**LEG DOVETAIL
TEMPLATE #4**

1 1/8"

11/16"
hinge mortise

4 11/16"

3 5/16"

Enlarge pattern 200% for full size

NOTE: Use a 1/4"
round-over on all interior
edges, top and bottom

INSIDE THE BOTTOM

photos by Kevin Dilley for Hazen Photography

Daru Stevens's "Step Chest & Sculpture, 'The Guardian'"
gallery piece, pau ferro, birdseye maple, maple, cherry,
teak, and purpleheart

The drawers lock when they are closed,
and it is not obvious how to open them.
Daru provides a card that reads, "To open
the drawers, the key is in the sculpture and
the directions are in the top drawer. Slide
the sculpture, jiggle the drawers. A little
click will tell you." There is a steel pin
under the treads on the left side of each
drawer that drops into place when the
drawer is shut. There is a large magnet
under the sculpture (and, incidentally, a
4" x 6" piece of steel out of sight under
the tread the sculpture is sitting on which
makes it feel heavy to pick up), that pulls
the pin up when placed in the right
position. The pin also locks it open, and
when raised, the drawer can be removed.

photo by Dan Fitzpatrick

Hal Taylor

Woodworking has been Hal Taylor's hobby all of his life with both his father and grandfather being fine craftsmen. Hal's first designs were concert quality classical guitars. Then, five years ago, Hal made a rocking chair for his daughter's second birthday. This was his first attempt at making chairs, but when he finished, he liked it so much he began to make more. With each one, he came up with more and more innovations to enhance the beauty and comfort of the chair. Hal has been making museum quality rocking chairs full-time now for two years.

"My intent when I started was to produce a product of unparalleled quality that was as much a work of art as it was a functional piece of furniture, keeping foremost in the design the concept that form should follow function. Recognizing that the function of a rocking chair is to provide a comfortable if not sensuous place to rest, relax, and regenerate our bodies and minds, it would be poor art to have any aspect of the artistic endeavor impinge on one's comfort. Simply put, the foremost function of every stick of wood in the chair is to provide unparalleled comfort to the sitter."

Hal's chairs are marketed at fine craft fairs and galleries in Virginia, Maryland, and Washington D.C.

Those who have had the chance to sit in one of Hal's chairs agree that it is the most comfortable chair they have ever sat in.

photo by Dan Fitzpatrick

Hal Taylor's Rocking Chair,
walnut with cherry accents,
41" L x 26" W x 41" H

This chair belongs to Dave Matthews of the Dave Matthews Band.

Rocking Chair

At least seven different routers are used to make these rocking chairs. Each is set up for a specific operation to save time.

Construction:

1. Select and prepare to size wood for the back legs, head rest, and seat. Cut the rear legs to exact size and shape with the bandsaw. Glue, surface, and square the seat. Cut two 3" x 3" corner notches in the seat to receive the long, rear legs. Rabbet these notches, top and bottom, with a router. See **Photo No. 1**.

2. Rout the seat notches to receive the front legs, using a jig that provides consistent sized openings. See **Photo No. 2**. Contouring the seat requires much handwork—shaping and smoothing. Cut the back leg joints on their two surfaces to match the rabbeted notches. The corners of the legs must also be radiused to match the routed rabbets of the seat notches. Shape the rear legs using special router table set-ups.

3. Form vertical back braces using a glue lamination process of three layers pressed over a prepared form or mold. Create the profile shapes of the back braces using a combination of band-sawing and routing. Form the perfectly round ends of the back braces with a ³⁄₁₆" round-over bit. Round-over the four edges with a trim router. To accommodate the curvatures of the back pieces, use a small laminate trim router fitted with a custom-made base. See **Trim Router diagram**. It has a convex surface and a zero clearance opening around the bit which allows for following all the contours and creating a uniform cut throughout.

4. Shape the front legs and rockers with round-over bits.

Photo No. 1.   Rabbeted notches cut in the seat to receive rear legs.

Photo No. 2.   With the seat supported vertically, the notching is router-cut for the front legs. Note waste backer clamped to the surface to prevent tear out.

Trim Router diagram

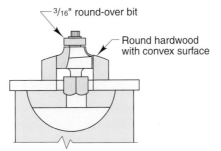

³⁄₁₆" round-over bit

Round hardwood with convex surface

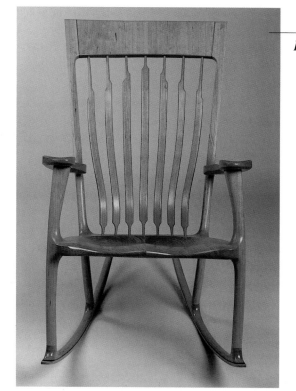

Hal Taylor's Rocking Chair, cherry with walnut accents

Hal Taylor's Rocking Chair, claro walnut

Hal Taylor's Rocking Chair arm detail,
cherry with walnut accents

photos by Dan Fitzpatrick

Hal Taylor's Rocking Chair,
maple with walnut accents

*Hal Taylor's Storytime
Chair, walnut*

*This chair was
designed to
accommodate the
three Taylor children,
Rachael, Aaron, and
Rose, during story-
time. In the place of
arms, Hal made two
little seats with backs
for the older children.*

photo by Fran Kirkendoll

Kim Taylor

Kim Taylor received an Associate Arts Degree in Millwork and Cabinetry from Sierra College, Rocklin, California in 1979. After graduation, Kim's mainstay of business was kitchen cabinetry and the occasional furniture piece. It was not long before his desire to do higher quality work pushed kitchens aside. He now concentrates solely on furniture; including tables, chairs, armoires, and entertainment centers.

For the past eight years, Kim has worked from his riverside studio workshop in Napa, California. The Napa Valley offers an excellent forum to exhibit his work in both galleries and wineries. He has participated in numerous individual and group exhibitions highlighted by "Natural Geometry," an individual show of his work at St. Supery Winery in the summer of 1994.

The "Angling West" line of tables is one of Kim's original designs in which the router is used extensively to produce the sliding dovetail joint between legs and aprons, as well as the inset of diamonds and arching aprons. This design works well with glass as well as slab tops. The tables are available in standard and custom sizes.

Angling West Tables

Construction:

1. Mill legs from 12/4 rough stock tapering from 2" x 2" at top to 2¾" x 2¾" at the bottom. See **Diagram No. 1**. Always square inside tapering out on the two outside surfaces. Heights vary: Coffee table, 17¼" ; End Table, 19¼"; and Sofa Table, 33¼". To rout the mortise in the leg, use the template guide method using a jig made of ⅛" aluminum that works from both ends to make both cuts from the same jig. See **Diagram No. 2**. The sliding dovetail mortise is 4" long and is chiseled square at the bottom.

2. Mill aprons from 6/4 rough stock to 1¼" thick. Rout the tenon, again using the template guide method on an aluminum plate jig. See **Diagram No. 3**. Aprons vary in length but are always 4½" at the tenon arching up to 3½" at center. Rough-cut the arch on the band saw and trim smooth by flush-routing with a template. Remove ½" from the bottom of the tenon with the band saw and chisel the mortise square to make a clean seat for the tenon.

3. Diamonds are ¾" x ¾" x ¼" beveled 45° and inlaid. The mortise is routed out with the router to ⅛" deep using the mortise jig. The corners are squared with a chisel.

4. Use ¾" thick starfire glass for table top.

photo by Jared Chandler

Angling West Tables diagram

Diagram No. 1.

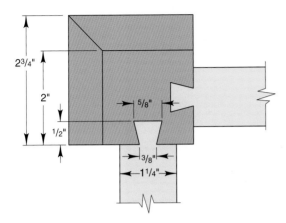

2 3/4"

2"

1/2"

5/8"

3/8"

1 1/4"

Diagram No. 2.

LEG MORTISE JIG

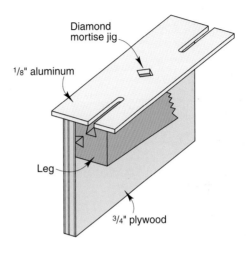

Diamond
mortise jig

1/8" aluminum

Leg

3/4" plywood

LEG

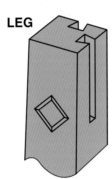

Diagram No. 3.

APRON TENON JIG

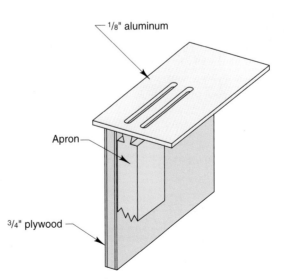

1/8" aluminum

Apron

3/4" plywood

APRON

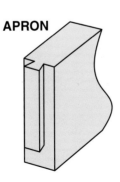

Kim Taylor's Coffee Table, walnut legs with maple aprons, 20" x 40" x 18" H

Kim Taylor's End Tables, walnut legs with maple aprons, 18" x 18" x 22" H

Kim Taylor's Sofa Table,
walnut legs with maple aprons,
15" x 60" x 34" H

photo by Jared Chandler

Kim Taylor's Table gallery piece,
maple, 34" x 68" x 30" H

Kim Taylor's Table gallery piece,
walnut, 45" x 90" x 30" H

photo by Gary McCarthy

where necessary. The clear finish is lacquer applied before assembly. The furniture is manually assembled with no heat, steam, glue, or other fasteners and can hold more than 700 pounds of weight.

Gregg Fleishman's Lumbarest, birch plywood, 24" W x 25" D x 43" H

Gregg Fleishman

Los Angeles artist and architect, Gregg Fleishman, received his Bachelor of Architecture from the University of Southern California n 1970. Since that time, he has worked on projects that combine artistic design with utility and comfort, something that he has accomplished with his "Lumbarest" chairs and other designs.

Gregg's idea was to achieve structural articulation by cutting away rather than joining pieces together. He spent more than four years evolutionizing his designs in which the wavelike springs act as both support surfaces and connecting elements. By experimenting with a variety of curved patterns, Gregg learned that different portions of the chair can be made to act in entirely different ways, for example, the frame remains fairly rigid while the seat and back are very "spring-like" and conform to the position of the sitter.

His chairs are created by routing slots in a toothlike pattern within a solid frame of ¾" European birch plywood. Edges and surfaces are finish-sanded

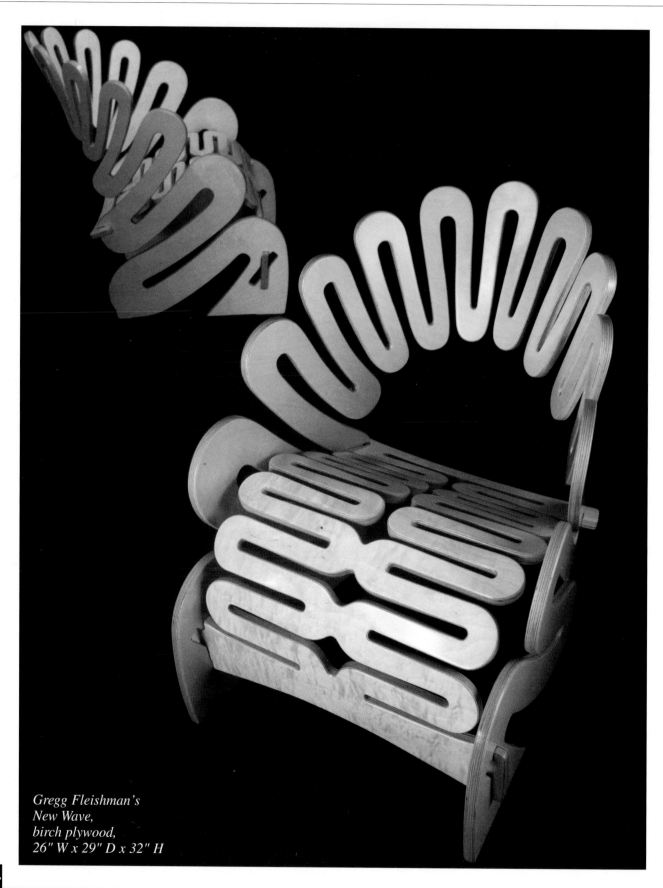

*Gregg Fleishman's
New Wave,
birch plywood,
26" W x 29" D x 32" H*

*Gregg Fleishman's Infinity pedestals,
birch plywood,
large: 24" W x 24" D x 29" H
small: 20" W x 20" D x 14" H*

*Gregg Fleishman's Alicia,
birch plywood, 24" W x 23" D x 34" H*

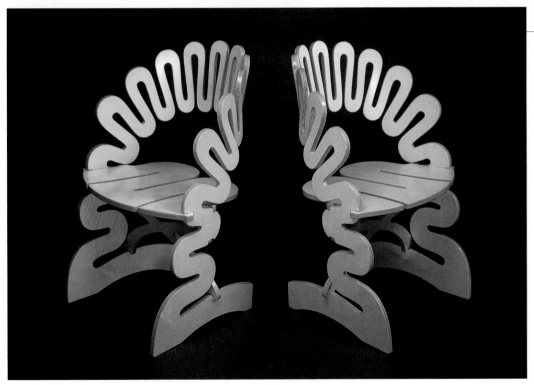

*Gregg
Fleishman's
Alicia,
birch plywood,
24" W x 23" D x
34" H*

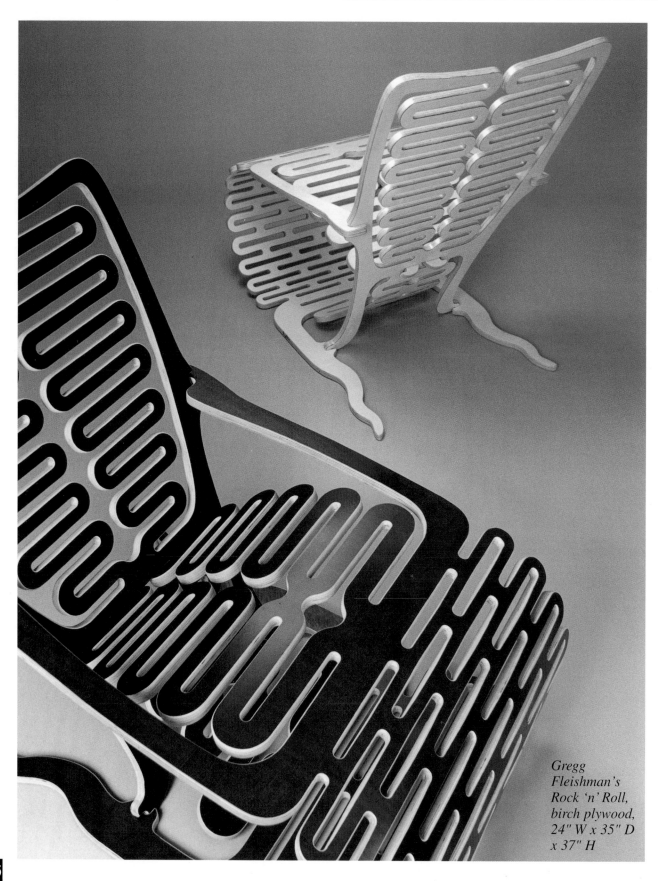

*Gregg
Fleishman's
Rock 'n' Roll,
birch plywood,
24" W x 35" D
x 37" H*

Monty Gould

Born and raised in Salt Lake City, Utah, Monty Gould first got a hint that he was artistically and mechanically inclined when he became a jeweler's apprentice while in high school.

For years Monty never pursued the artistic ability, perhaps he wasn't even certain it was there. But then at the age of 61, Monty started a new life with a new wife and a new "old" house. He learned he could do anything; wiring, plumbing, wallpapering, even learning to make stained glass so he could make a light fixture for his dining room.

For health reasons, Monty had to give up a lot of the things that use to give him pleasure, such as riding his Honda Gold Wing. But for everything he had to give up, he found something else that he could do to keep himself excited to start a new day. Such was the case when his hip started bothering him at age 75. He realized that he needed a cane, and if he had to use one, he wanted it to be a spectacular one. So, he started making canes and has never stopped.

Monty is now 80 years old and is constantly thinking up new patterns for his canes, both for the handles and the staffs. If he can visualize the pattern in his mind, he can produce it on his Woodchuck. He doesn't use stain, preferring to let the natural colors of the exotic woods shine through a clear varathane finish.

He was first introduced to the open spiral when he was repairing a piece of antique furniture. He incorporated this look into some of his canes and also into a line of spiral candlestick holders. He operates his business, Classy Canes, from his small "one car garage turned shop" at his home in Seattle.

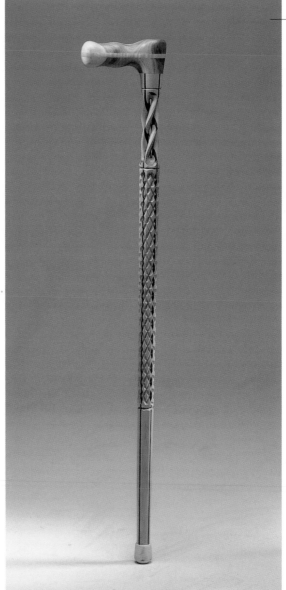

Monty Gould's Diamond Cane, Handle: canary, curly maple, Stick: sycamore, purpleheart

Twist was cut with a 1" rope router bit, followed by a ⅛" up-cut bit. Diamonds were cut with a ½" "V"-shaped bit.

photo by Kevin Dilley for Hazen Photography

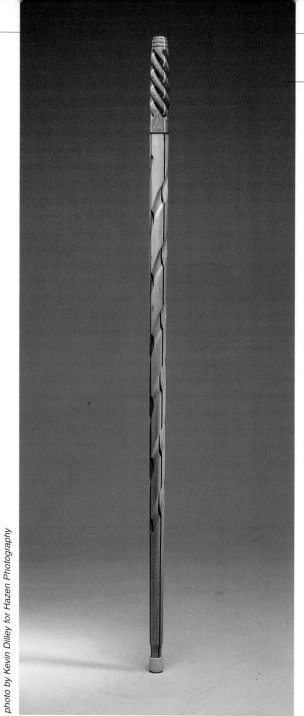

Monty Gould's Walking Stick
Handle: lacewood, maple plywood,
Stick: sycamore, purpleheart

Handle is cut using ¾" rope style router
bit followed by ⅛" straight up-cut bit.
Spiral on stick was cut using a 1½"
classic bit for spiral, and 2" flat router
bit for flat sides. All edges sanded.

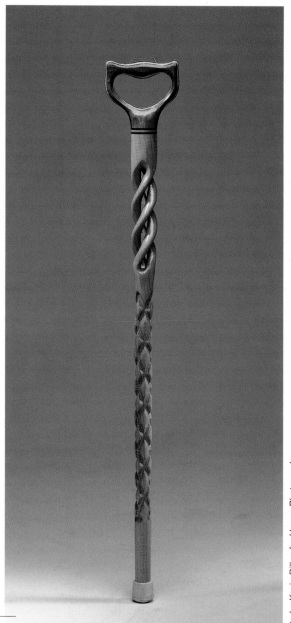

Monty Gould's Cat-faced or Shovel Cane,
Handle: satinwood, purpleheart, maple, walnut,
Tennessee (red) cedar, Stick: hard maple, purpleheart

Hollow twist made with a 2" round-over bit. Diamond
pattern was made with a ½" classic bit. After handle
was cut, shaped, and sanded, a ½" round-over bit was
used to round the edges on a router table.

*Monty Gould's Left-hand Palm Cane,
Handle: Laminated redheart, maple,
purpleheart, padouk, spalted maple,
Stick: curly maple*

*Spiral was cut with a 1" rope twist router
bit, followed by a ⁵⁄₃₂" straight up-cut bit to
complete the hollow. Line cuts made by ½"
classic bit. Cut made around the stick cut
with a 1" barley-twist bit. Lower half of
stick is 5-sided. Handle and stick are
attached with a ¾" purpleheart dowel.*

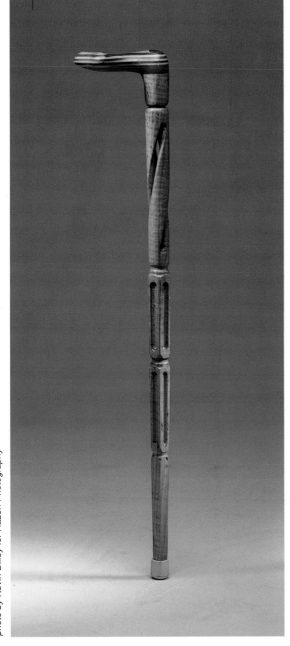

*Monty Gould's Candle Holder,
purpleheart hollow spirals, ash base
topped with ½" redheart, topped with
¼" apple.*

*Spiral cut with a 1½" rope-twist bit,
followed by a ⅛" straight up-cut bit.*

*The center base pieces of apple and
redheart were laminated and then
router-cut with a classic bit. The
bottom base piece of ash was also
router-cut with the same classic bit,
then the pieces were laminated.*

photo by Tim Barnwell

Ray Jones

Ray Jones was raised in a small town in Northern California. During the summer months of his college years, he worked as a construction laborer/ carpenter's assistant. After obtaining a degree in Aeronautical Engineering in 1976 from California Polytechnic State University, he moved to Southern California to work for an aerospace propulsion firm. When setting up his first household, he bought tools instead

of furniture, and then proceeded to build his furniture. Once his home was furnished, he turned his woodworking attention to making gifts, including a unique jewelry box for his future wife. This box design became the foundation of his woodworking career which began in 1982 when he left his engineering job. Since then, he has been making wood boxes full-time and selling them through galleries and craft fairs. He now lives in Western North Carolina with his wife, Linda, and their three children.

"I believe that a wood box should be just that—wood. So, as much as possible, I use only wood in my boxes, including the fasteners, hinges, and drawer slides. I am fascinated by wooden mechanisms, and the intersections of various geometric shapes."

"I am also intrigued by the tremendous variety of woods that exist in the world. While trying to use sustainable harvested, plantation grown, salvaged, or otherwise 'environmentally friendly' species, my inventory has grown to more than forty types of wood. These range from some of the highly-figured but rarely seen West Coast varieties, to lesser known species from planned forestry projects in Mexico and South America, to tropical exotics salvaged in the Florida Keys."

In the last six years, Ray has been featured in numerous exhibitions and won many awards, most recently Best of Show and People's Choice at the 1996 Northwest Fine Woodworking Annual Box Competition in Seattle, Washington.

*Ray Jones' Box,
birdseye maple
and purpleheart,
15" x 9" x 4¼"*

photo by Tim Barnwell

The box is straight forward construction with the rounded front hand-shaped following rough bandsawing. With the router installed in a table, a spiral pattern bit is used with a fixture which holds the box front at 45° and provides a half-circle pattern for the finger recesses. Another fixture is used for the slots in the drawer fronts, though this one holds the work piece perpendicular to the router's axis. The router table is also used to make rabbets in the bottom and sides of the drawer-fronts. A dovetail bit is used to cut slots in the top of the box bottom to center guide each drawer slide.

For the trays and drawer sides, a custom-made bit is used to cut the finger joints. This bit is essentially three slot cutters on an arbor with spacers. This allows for cutting all the fingers on a stack of pieces, clamped in a sliding table arrangement, in a single pass.

photo by Tim Barnwell

*Ray Jones' Telephone,
curly koa, dogwood,
and Maccassar ebony,
9" x 8½" x 4½"*

The wood body replaces the housing of a purchased phone. The components fit in from the bottom. For the phone's handset, a jig was made that clamps to the router table and holds the router with its axis horizontal. Then two fixtures were made that could mount in a cross-slide vise, also clamped to the router table. This became a horizontal milling machine. One fixture rotates the stock in a single plane, whose angle to the router axis is set by the relationship of the vise to the router

*Ray Jones'
Telephone handset
variation, chechen*

jig. This same set-up was used with a dish-cutter bit to make the recesses in the phone body in which the handset rests.

The second fixture rotates the work piece as it is moved axially at a proportional rate. This fixture was used with a thread cutter bit to cut the female threads on the receiver ends. This could have also been used for the male threads as well, but Ray chose to do them on the lathe, since the mouth and ear cups were turned anyway.

For the dovetail splines in the phone body, the router was mounted in the table with a dovetail bit, and a sliding jig was made to hold the phone body inverted at a 45° angle to the router axis.

Barry LaChance

Barry LaChance began his furniture making career out of necessity. After moving to the Houston area in 1971 he needed to furnish his apartment, and it was cheaper to build than to buy. He has come a long way since those days, becoming a highly skilled woodsmith and noted collector of fine antiques.

Barry's days were spent as an environmental engineer for Lockheed at NASA, just south of Houston. At night, he became a musician and the front man for a well-known local band—an avocation that was becoming a vocation. Another avocation was also demanding more and more of his time—woodworking. A friend with a "shop full of tools" showed him the basics, and, by 1977, it was time to leave Lockheed and ply his twin avocations full time.

The Wood Works, a wood shop as unique as the fine furniture that issues from its doors, was the result. On a typical day, half of Barry's workforce are skilled professional cabinet makers; the other half are his "apprentices"—retired managers and professionals from the oil and aerospace industries. Their only pay is the satisfaction they draw from the wood, developing their own skills, and the use of an almost unlimited array of woodworking tools.

Barry designs his furniture to suit his own tastes which run to late 19th century style and decoration. Thus his pieces are often termed as "eclectic Victorian" because Barry chooses his forms and decoration from a wide range of options. The only thing his furniture has never been called is "dull."

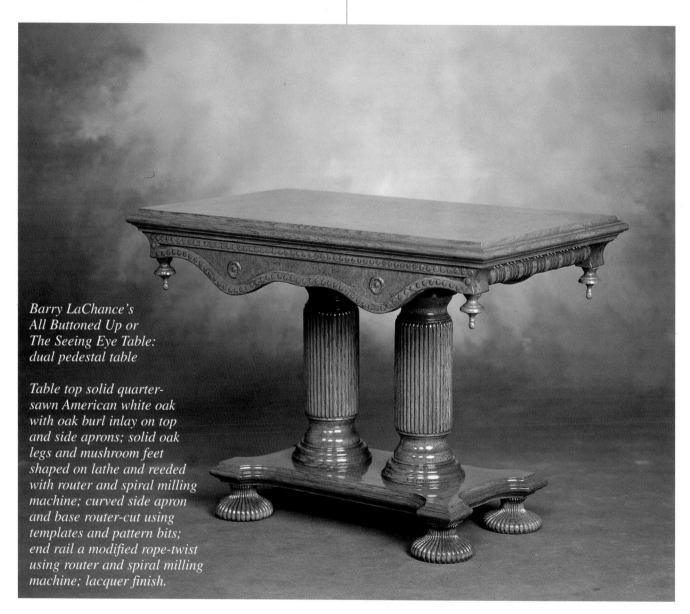

Barry LaChance's All Buttoned Up or The Seeing Eye Table: dual pedestal table

Table top solid quarter-sawn American white oak with oak burl inlay on top and side aprons; solid oak legs and mushroom feet shaped on lathe and reeded with router and spiral milling machine; curved side apron and base router-cut using templates and pattern bits; end rail a modified rope-twist using router and spiral milling machine; lacquer finish.

On page 133: Barry LaChance's Not So Paltry Hall Tree: hall tree

Solid American white oak throughout; primary flat surfaces inlaid with oak burl veneer; others veneered with flaky oak; feet, columns, and interrupted columns reeded or fluted using router and spiral milling machine; all moldings router-cut using French Provincial and other assorted bits; copper lined umbrella catch; drawers with handmade dovetails and ebony drawer pulls; lacquer finish.

Barry LaChance's Éntagere: étagère with enclosed entertainment center

Solid Honduras mahogany throughout; all concave surfaces routed with core box bit using templates on pin router and veneered with pommele sapele; all turnings on lathe and reeded with router and spiral milling machine; TV cabinet doors and accent panels veneered in crotch mahogany; other flat surfaces veneered in pommele sapele; moldings routed using various round-over and French Provincial bits; deck is of solid Empress Verde Light marble; lacquer finish.

Barry LaChance's No Cabinet Is An Island: kitchen island cabinet

Features four useable sides with decorative removable center support for upper cabinet to increase working area of solid granite counter top; fluted columns at corners of lower cabinet and ¼" round rope twist at upper cabinet corners (both using router and spiral milling machine), custom leaded glass in all doors; door stiles fluted using router; decorative brackets cut with router pattern bit following templates.

A.C. (Al) Pihlaja

A. C. (Al) Pihlaja is a retired electrical engineer living in Portland, Oregon. Al credits his eighth grade woodshop teacher for getting him interested in wood-working, a hobby that has lasted many, many years. Raising four children left Al with many opportunities to build lots of toys, furniture, and canoes; then when his family grew with two stepsons, and later with thirteen grandchildren and two great-grandchildren, his hobby just had to grow too.

The idea of the Pirate's Chest was conceived when his six year old grandson became interested in pirates and begged him to go looking for buried treasure. Grandpa came through by designing and building a chest and even burying it in the sand so they could go on their treasure hunt.

Both the router and Kellar's Dovetail System were instrumental in the making of the chest. The top boards were first mitered to fit the curved top and then dovetailed.

Al's main interest is creating furniture pieces where he can apply all of his skills and incorporate all of his shop equipment. Al spends many happy hours in his shop and says, "no man should be permitted to have so much fun."

A.C. Pihlaja's Pirate's Chest, red oak, 12" D x 13" H x 18" L

photo by Kevin Dilley for Hazen Photography

A.C. Pihlaja's Pirate's Chest open,
red oak, 12" D x 13" H x 18" L

photo by Kevin Dilley for Hazen Photography

photo by Jim McHugh

Pat Warner

Pat Warner is a self taught designer-craftsman and teaches routing at Palomar Community College in San Marcos, California. Most of his work is experimental. He uses the router for edge jointing, template making, decorative and excavational work, fabricating precision jigs and fixtures, and it is his primary joinery tool.

"Like most of the work I do, this desk was an experiment. I wanted a variation of a pedestal desk but wondered if I couldn't hang the pedestals off the underside of the top rather than have the top rest on the pedestals. The design advantage of such a structure is that the pedestals, (now drawer boxes) could be essentially any size since they needn't support the top. I could have one on either or both sides. For balance, the rail below the top can be the front of a pencil drawer (as in my case) or just a rail.

"The drawer boxes in the featured desk are structural. The end assemblies by themselves can support the top but they do not offer any resistance to sideways forces. The drawer box stiffens the desk up nicely.

The top is a full thickness tongue and groove complimentary routed decoration. It was made in three sections, two of oak and one of mahogany."

Pat is the author of a trilogy of routing books: *Getting The Very Best From Your Router*, 1996; *Router Joinery*, scheduled release 1997; and *Router Jigs and Fixtures*, scheduled release 1998. He is also a frequent contributor to *Fine Woodworking* and *Woodwork* magazines.

Pat has designed, and is the manufacturer of, the clear plastic router offset bases for both the Porter Cable Corp. and DeWalt Industrial Tool Company. He makes his home in Escondido, California.

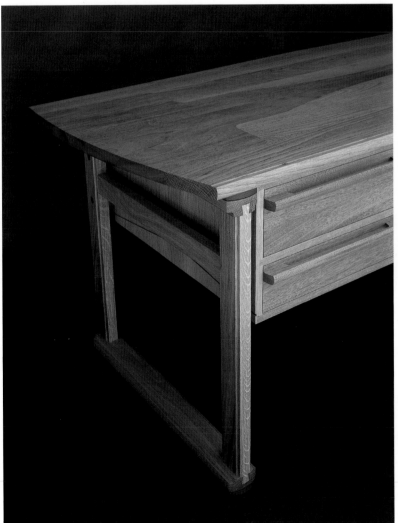

photo by Curtis B. Wilson, MD

Pat Warner's Desk,
Honduras mahogany and white oak,
75" L x 29" W x 29½" H

Pat Warner's Desk,
Honduras mahogany and white oak,
75" L x 29" W x 29½" H

Pat Warner's Coffee Table,
jatoba and walnut,
59" x 19½" x 17" H

Pat Warner's Coffee Table,
jatoba and walnut,
59" x 19½" x 17" H

Pat Warner's Coffee Table
joint on underside,
jatoba and walnut,
59" x 19½" x 17" H

The aluminum plate
resides in a sloppy mortise.
It fastens the top to the
rail. The screw slides in a
slot in the plate for
seasonal width changes.

Metric Conversion Chart

mm-millimetres   cm-centimetres
inches to millimetres and centimetres

inches	mm	cm	inches	cm	inches	cm
⅛	3	0.3	9	22.9	30	76.2
¼	6	0.6	10	25.4	31	78.7
½	13	1.3	12	30.5	33	83.8
⅝	16	1.6	13	33.0	34	86.4
¾	19	1.9	14	35.6	35	88.9
⅞	22	2.2	15	38.1	36	91.4
1	25	2.5	16	40.6	37	94.0
1¼	32	3.2	17	43.2	38	96.5
1½	38	3.8	18	45.7	39	99.1
1¾	44	4.4	19	48.3	40	101.6
2	51	5.1	20	50.8	41	104.1
2½	64	6.4	21	53.3	42	106.7
3	76	7.6	22	55.9	43	109.2
3½	89	8.9	23	58.4	44	111.8
4	102	10.2	24	61.0	45	114.3
4½	114	11.4	25	63.5	46	116.8
5	127	12.7	26	66.0	47	119.4
6	152	15.2	27	68.6	48	121.9
7	178	17.8	28	71.1	49	124.5
8	203	20.3	29	73.7	50	127.0

yards to metres

yards	metres	yards	metres	yards	metres	yards	metres	yards	metres
⅛	0.11	2⅛	1.94	4⅛	3.77	6⅛	5.60	8⅛	7.43
¼	0.23	2¼	2.06	4¼	3.89	6¼	5.72	8¼	7.54
⅜	0.34	2⅜	2.17	4⅜	4.00	6⅜	5.83	8⅜	7.66
½	0.46	2½	2.29	4½	4.11	6½	5.94	8½	.7.77
⅝	0.57	2⅝	2.40	4⅝	4.23	6⅝	6.06	8⅝	7.89
¾	0.69	2¾	2.51	4¾	4.34	6¾	6.17	8¾	8.00
⅞	0.80	2⅞	2.63	4⅞	4.46	6⅞	6.29	8⅞	8.12
1	0.91	3	2.74	5	4.57	7	6.40	9	8.23
1⅛	1.03	3⅛	2.86	5⅛	4.69	7⅛	6.52	9⅛	8.34
1¼	1.14	3¼	2.97	5¼	4.80	7¼	6.63	9¼	8.46
1⅜	1.26	3⅜	3.09	5⅜	4.91	7⅜	6.74	9⅜	8.57
1½	1.37	3½	3.20	5½	5.03	7½	6.86	9½	8.69
1⅝	1.49	3⅝	3.31	5⅝	5.14	7⅝	6.97	9⅝	8.80
1¾	1.60	3¾	3.43	5¾	5.26	7¾	7.09	9¾	8.92
1⅞	1.71	3⅞	3.54	5⅞	5.37	7⅞	7.20	9⅞	9.03
2	1.83	4	3.66	6	5.49	8	7.32	10	9.14

Index

photo by Raeff Miles, Vancouver, Canada